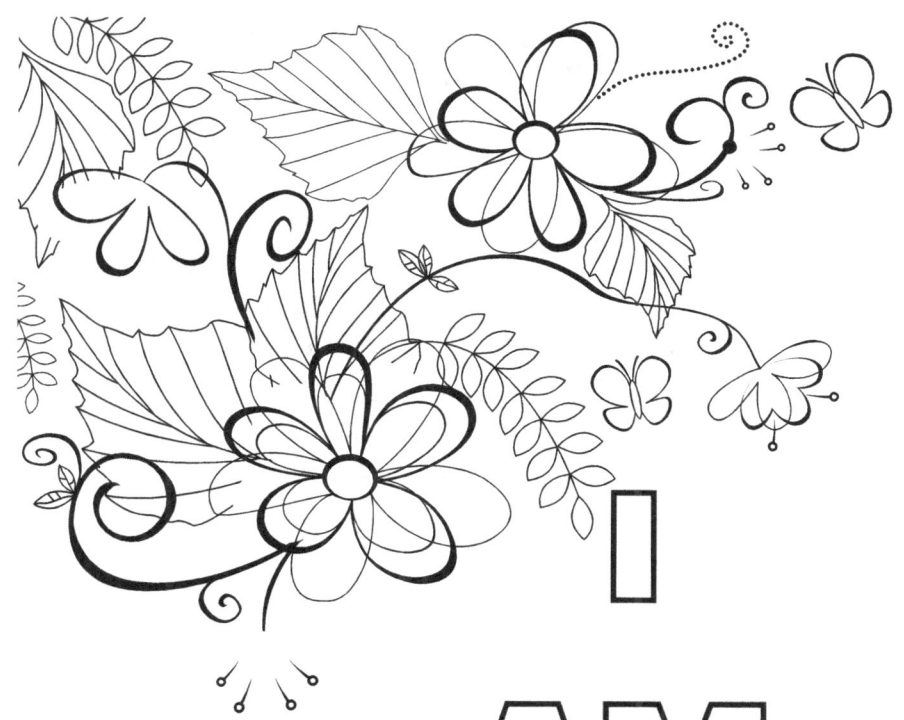

I AM ENOUGH!

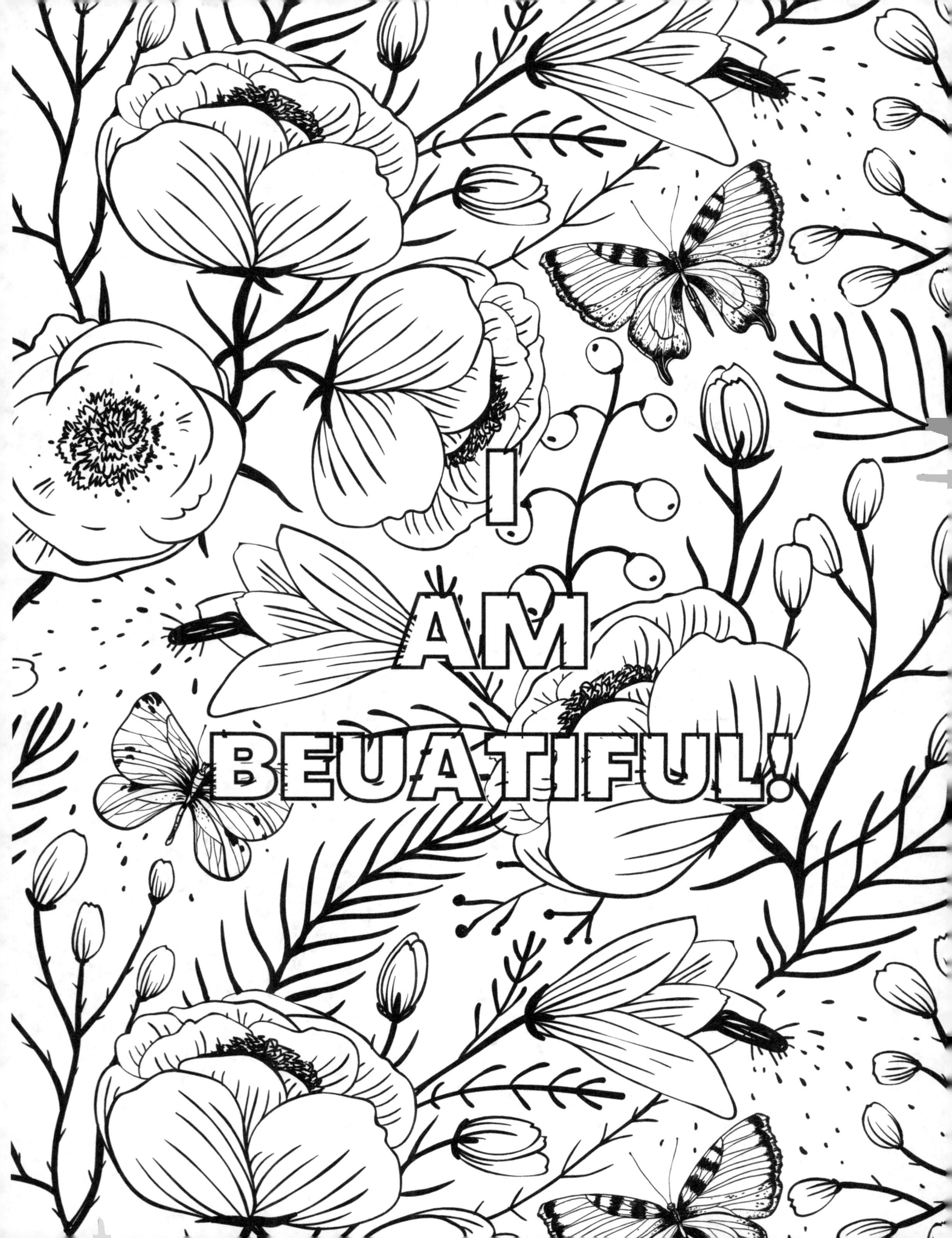

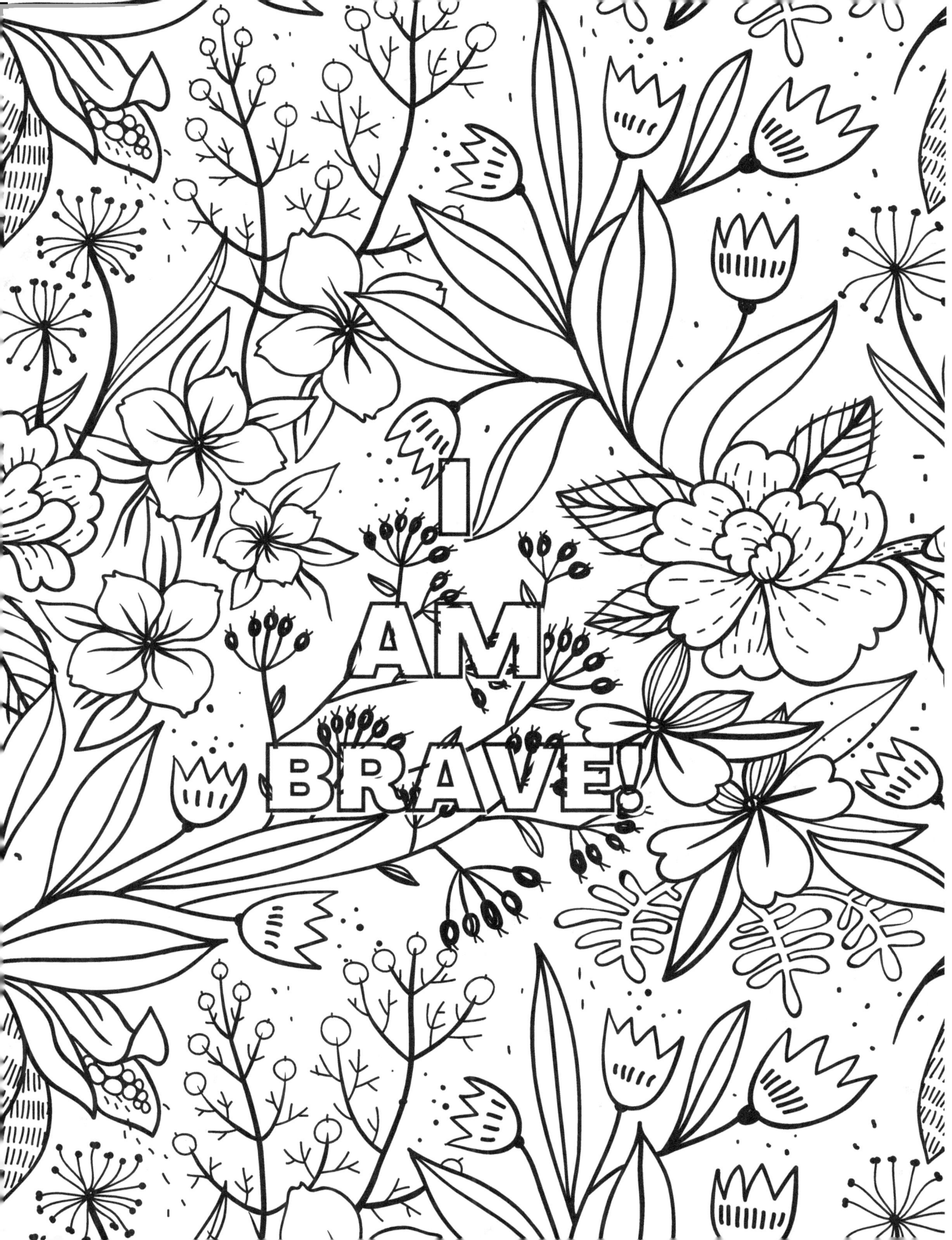

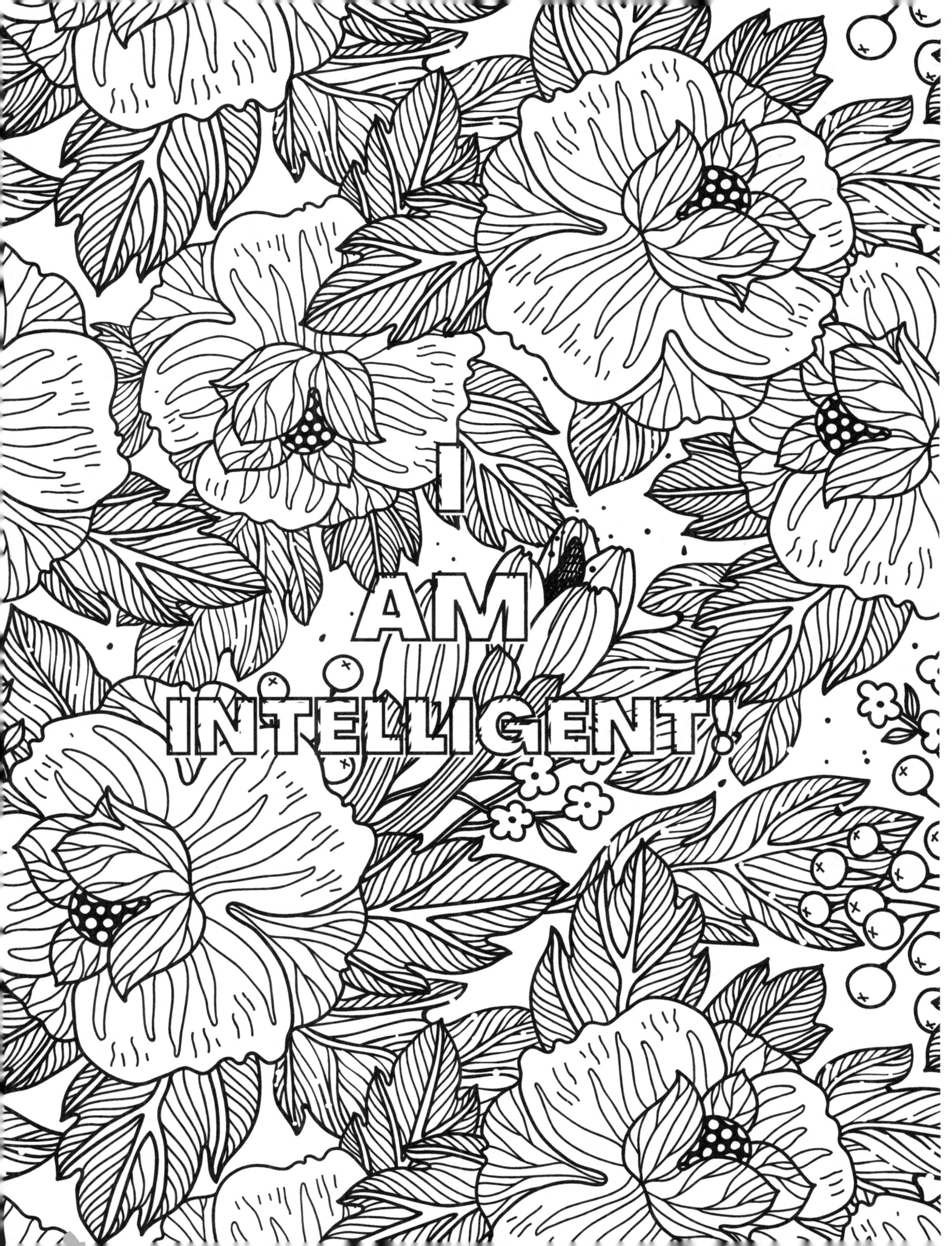

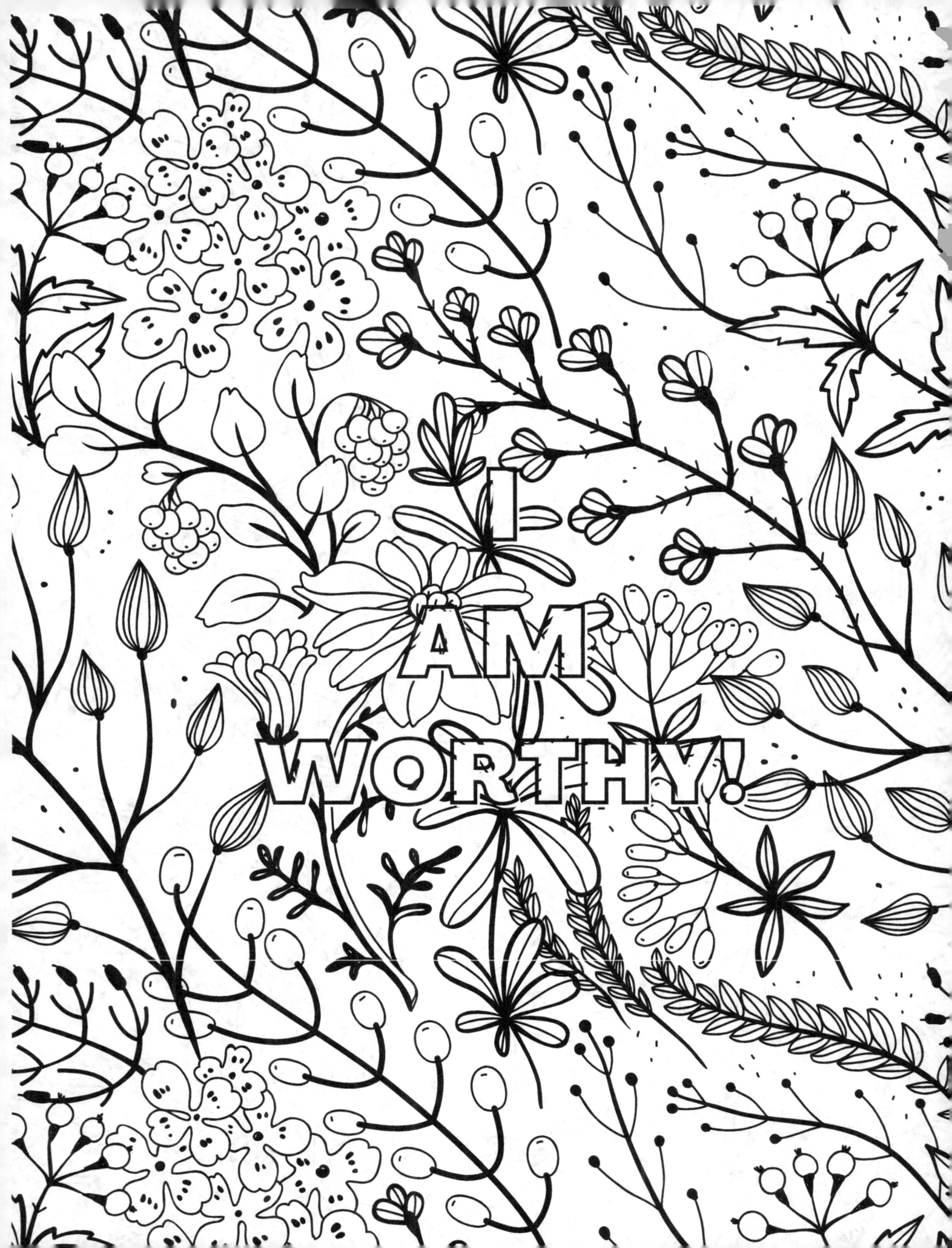

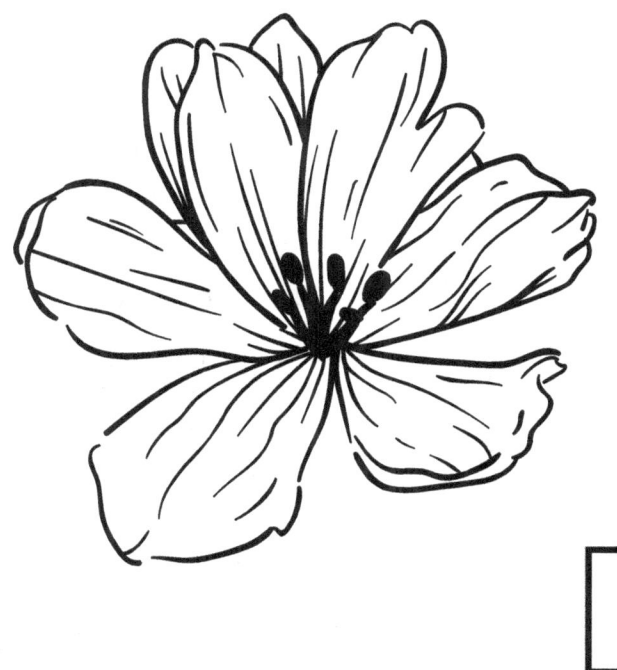

I
AM
LOVED!

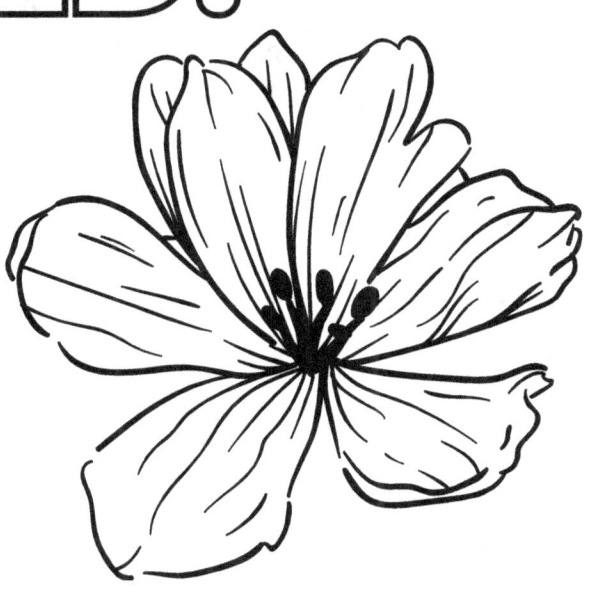

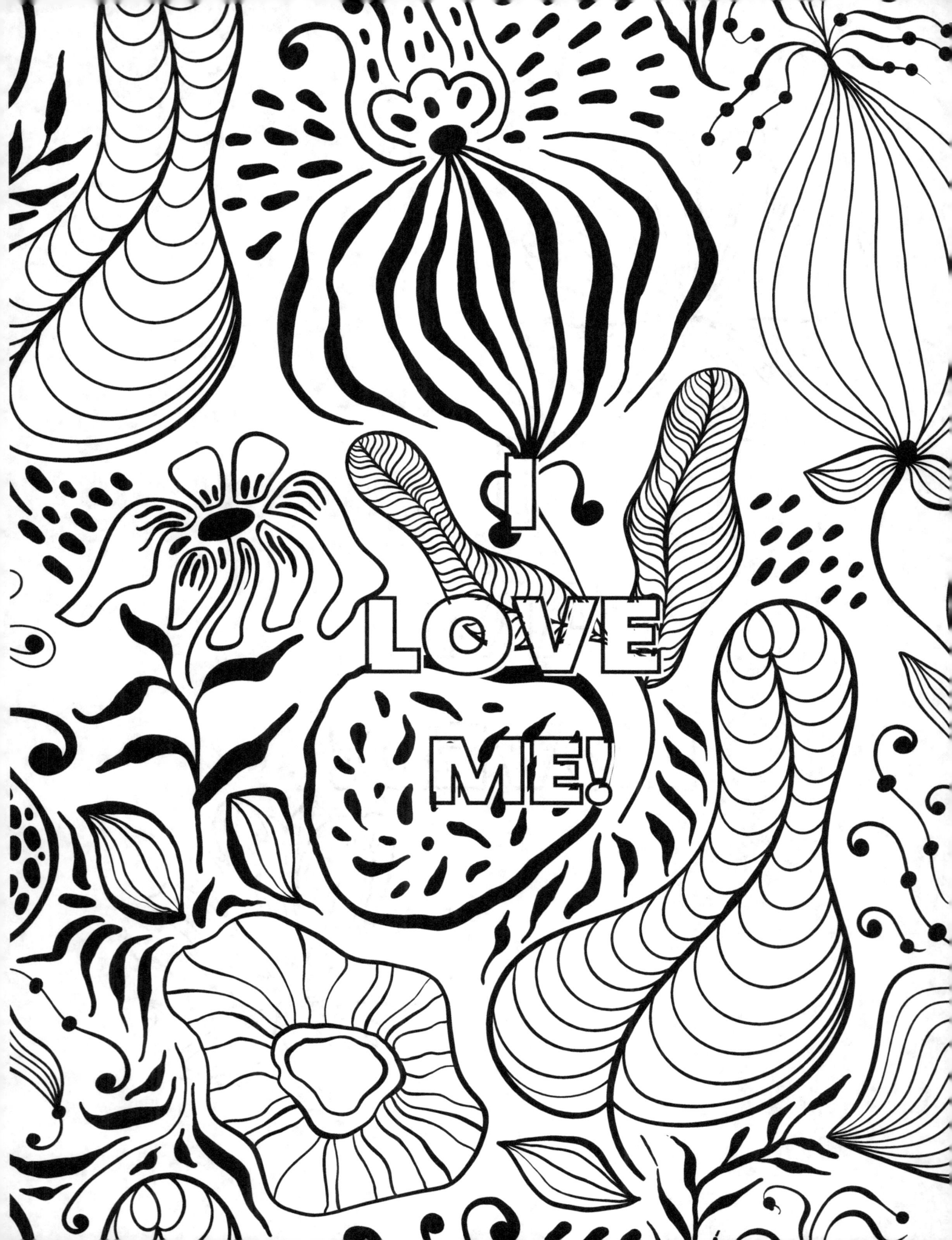

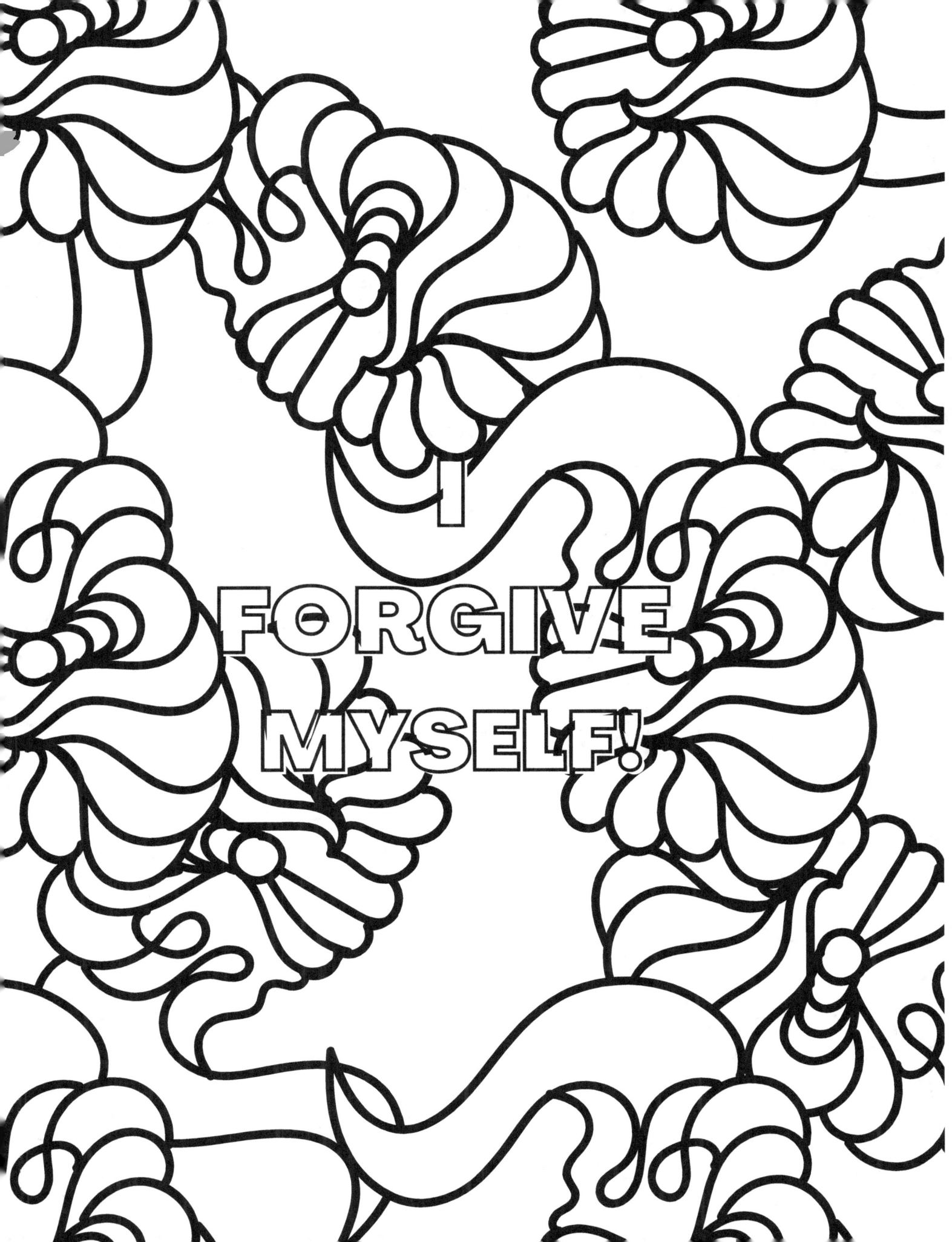

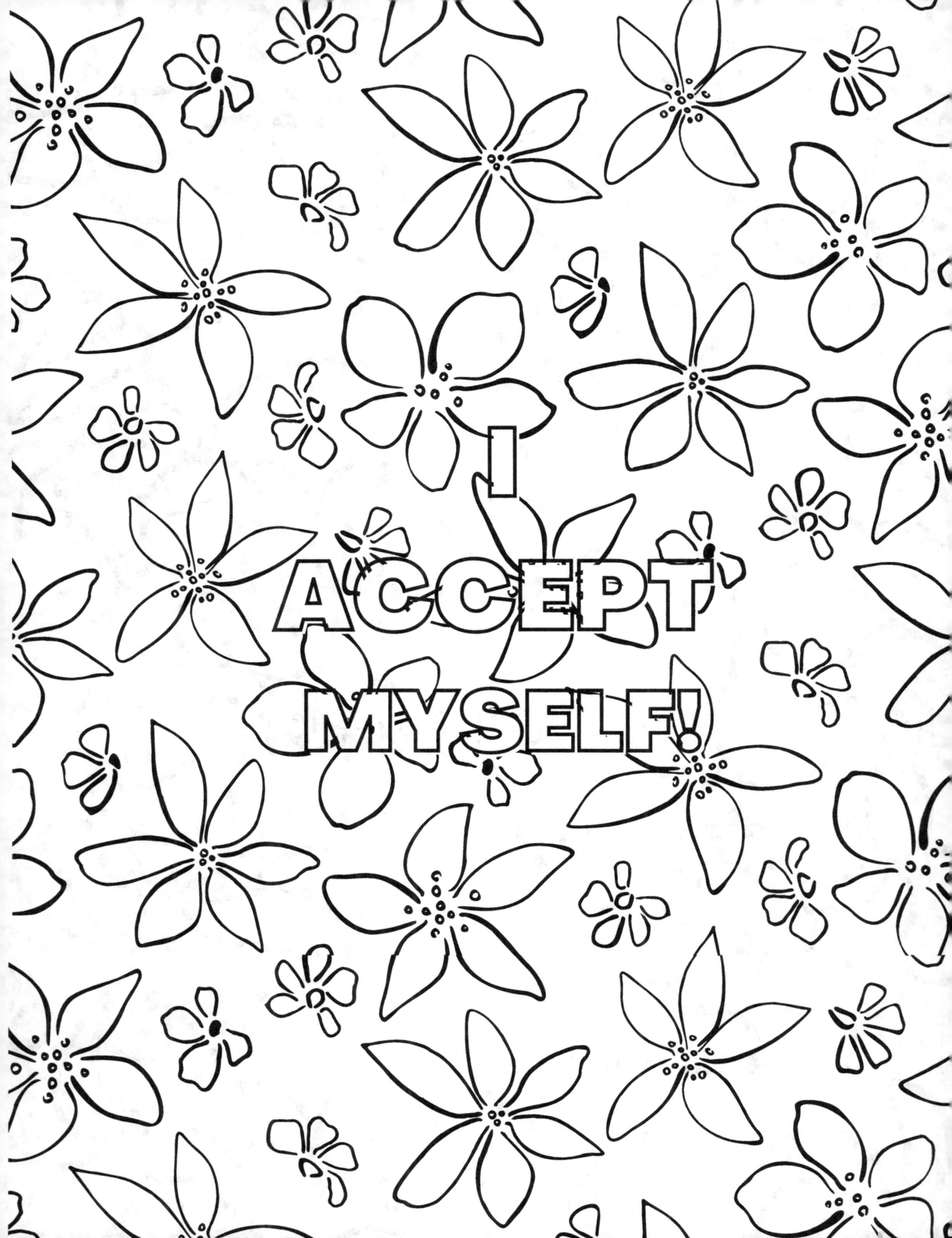

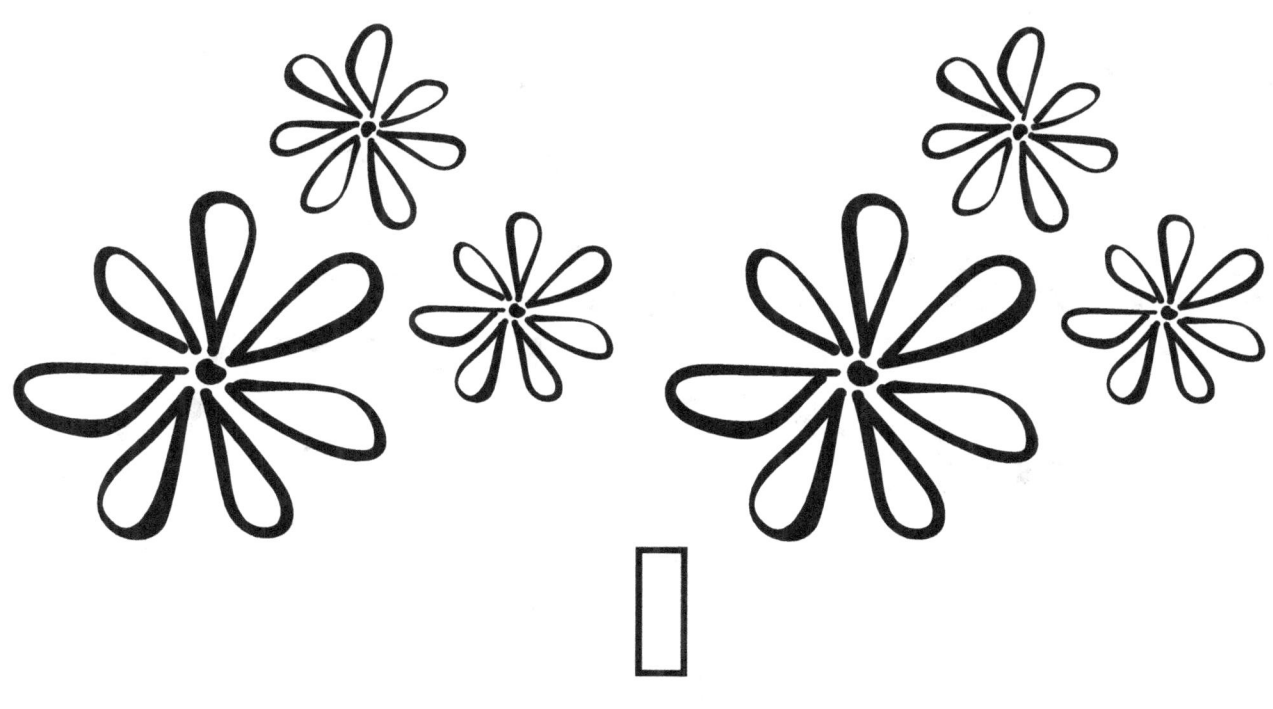

I
AM
FLEXIBLE!

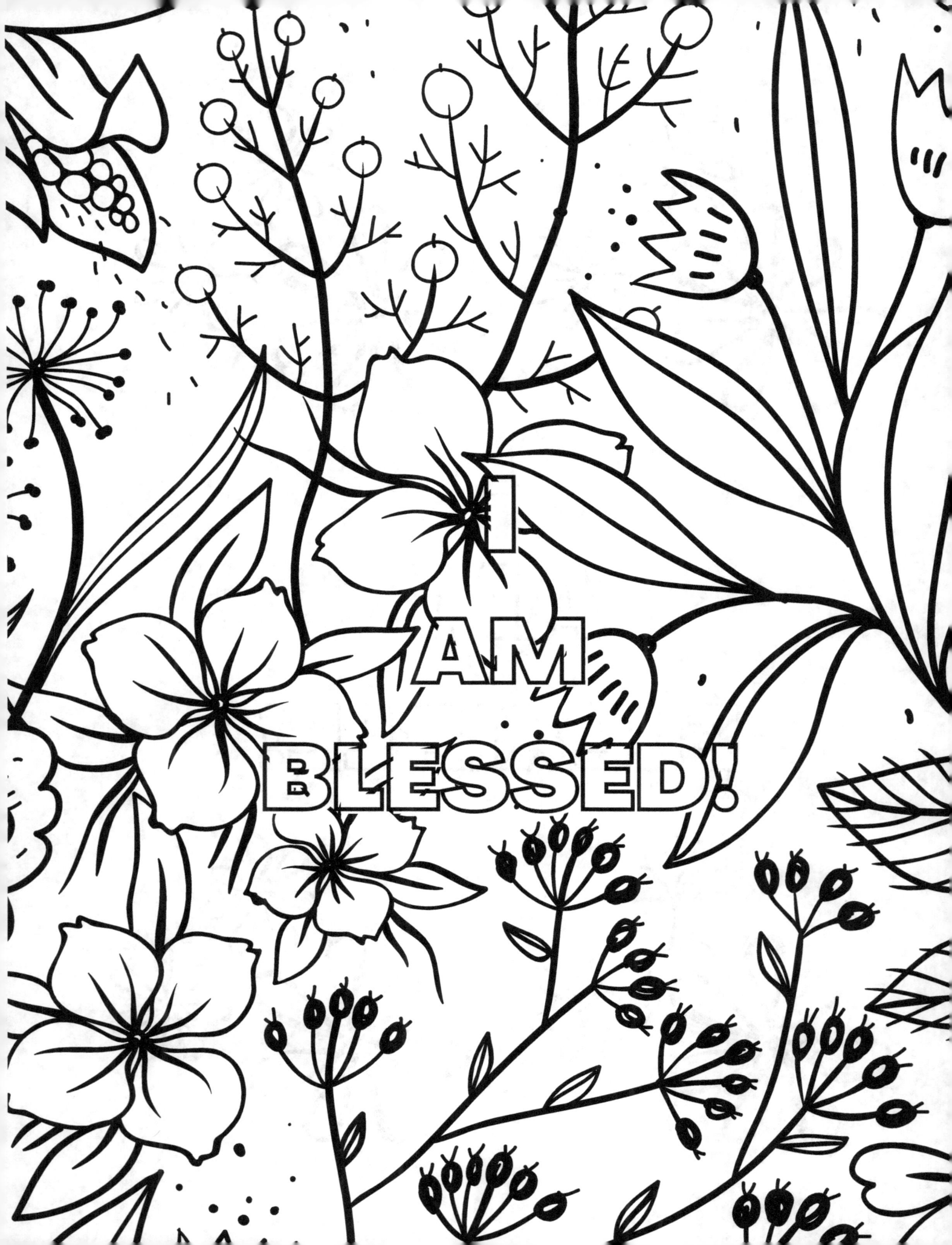

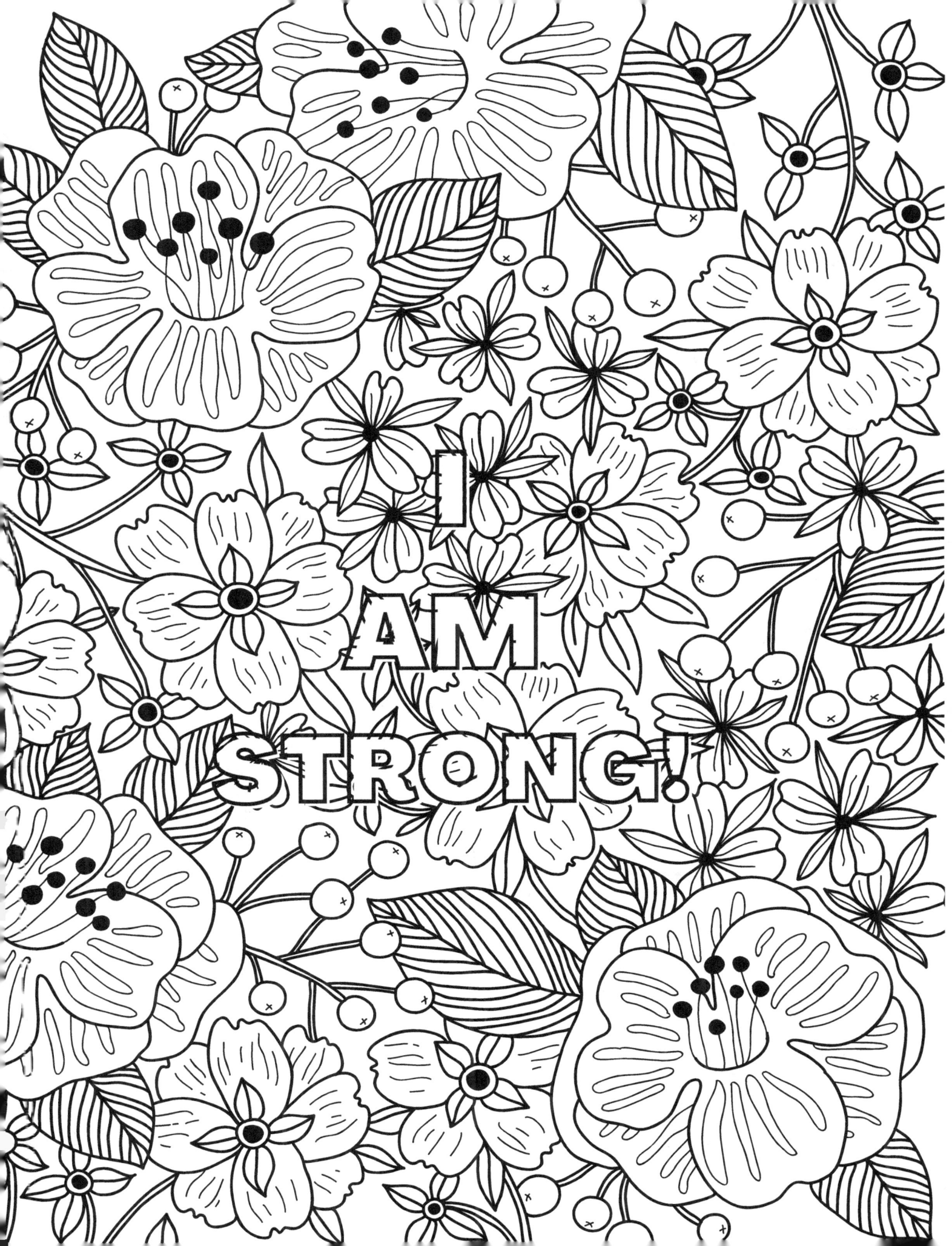

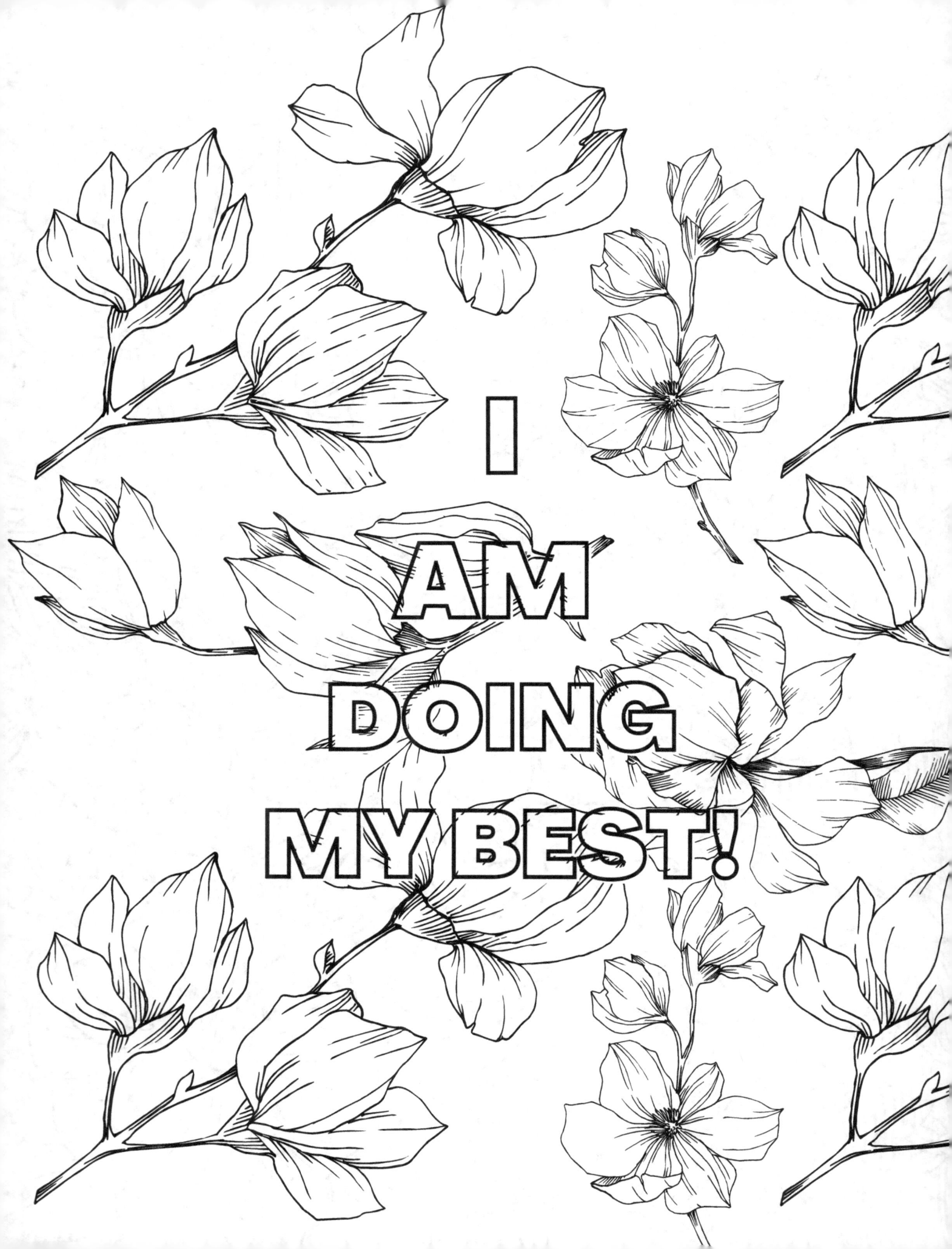

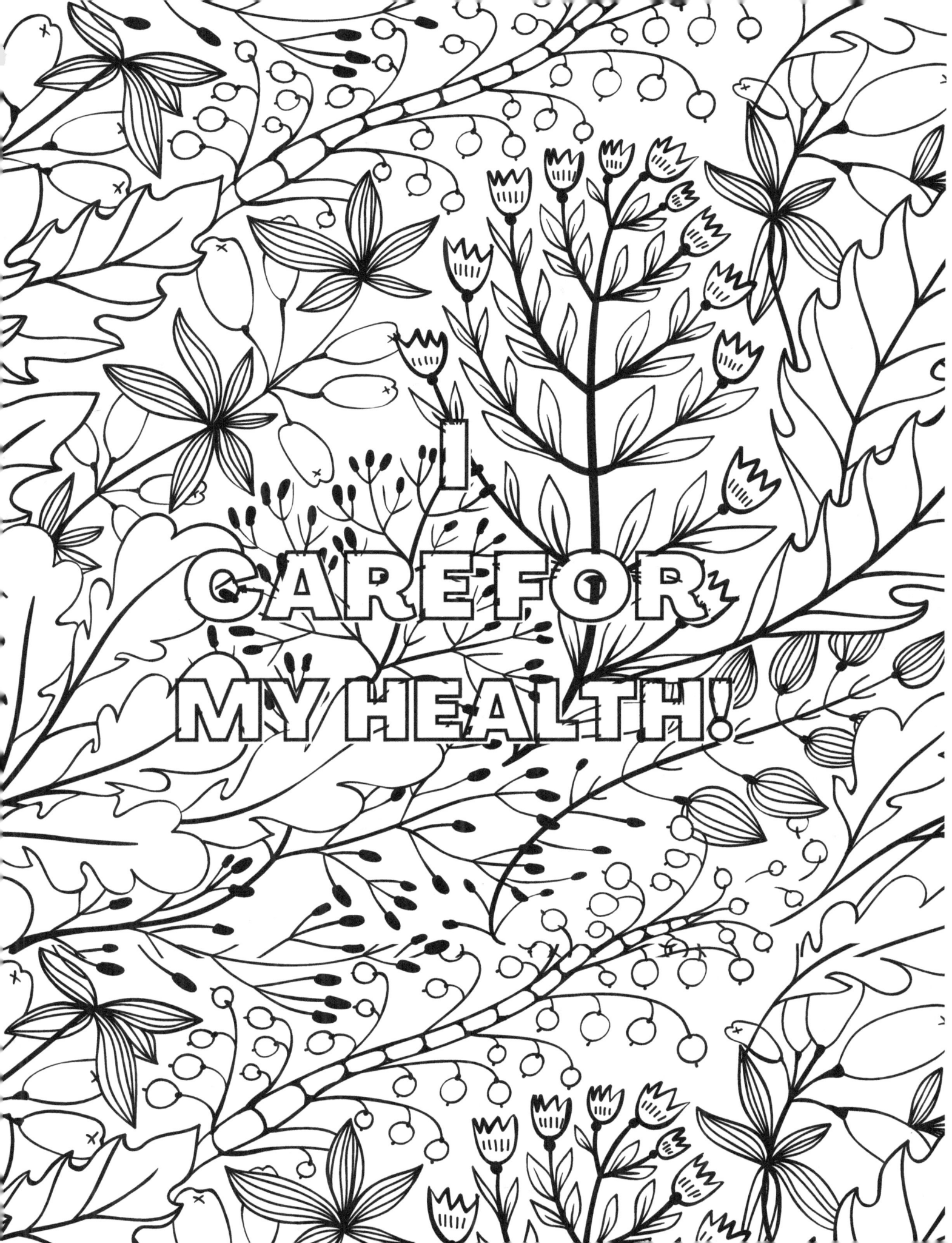

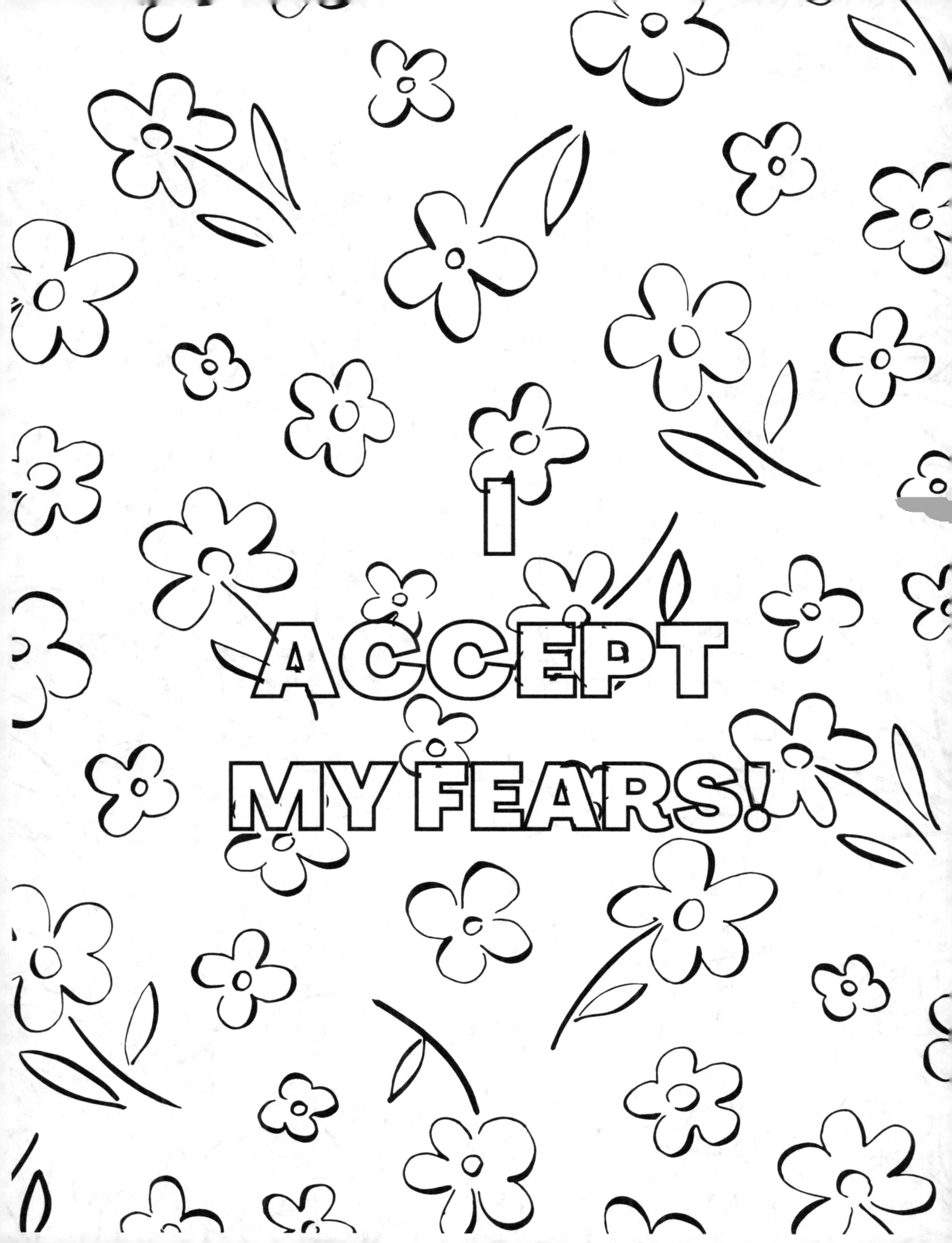

I RESPECT ME!

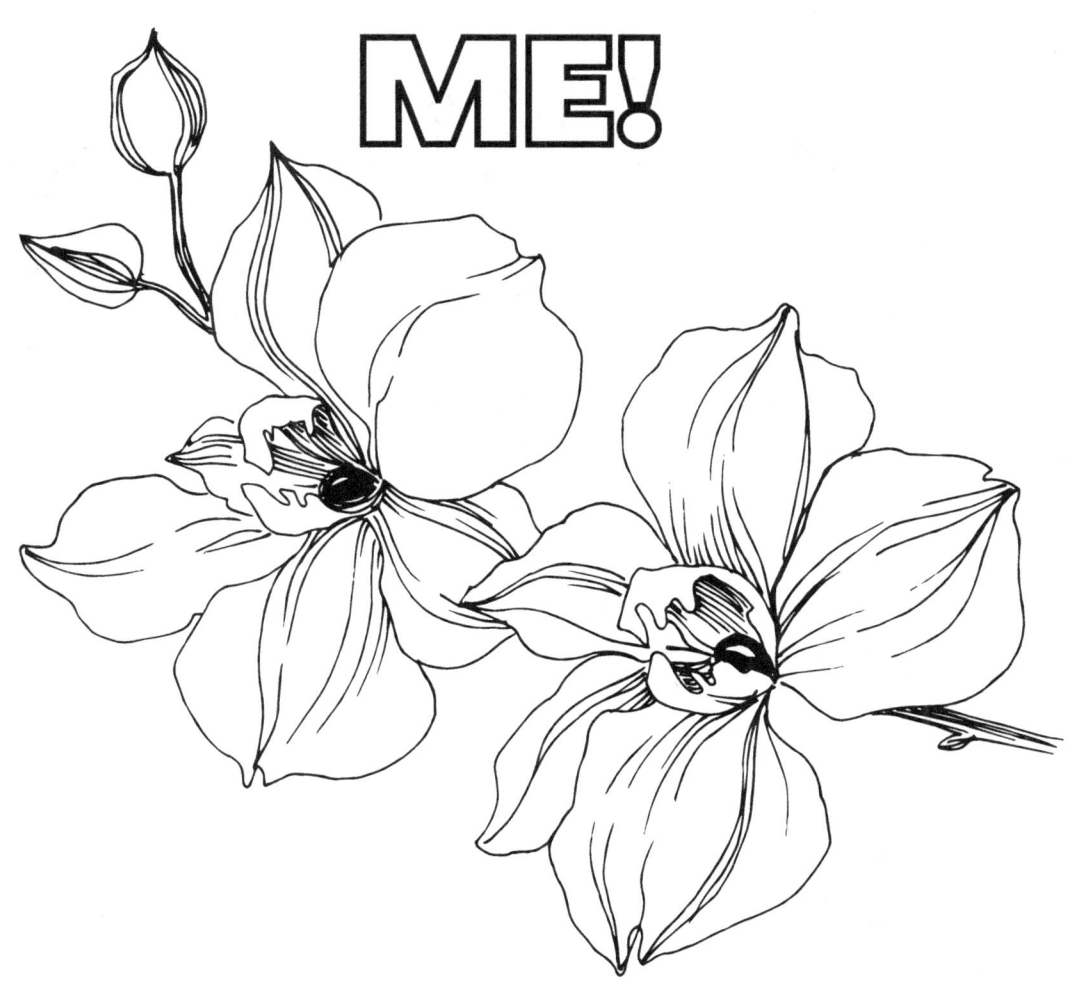

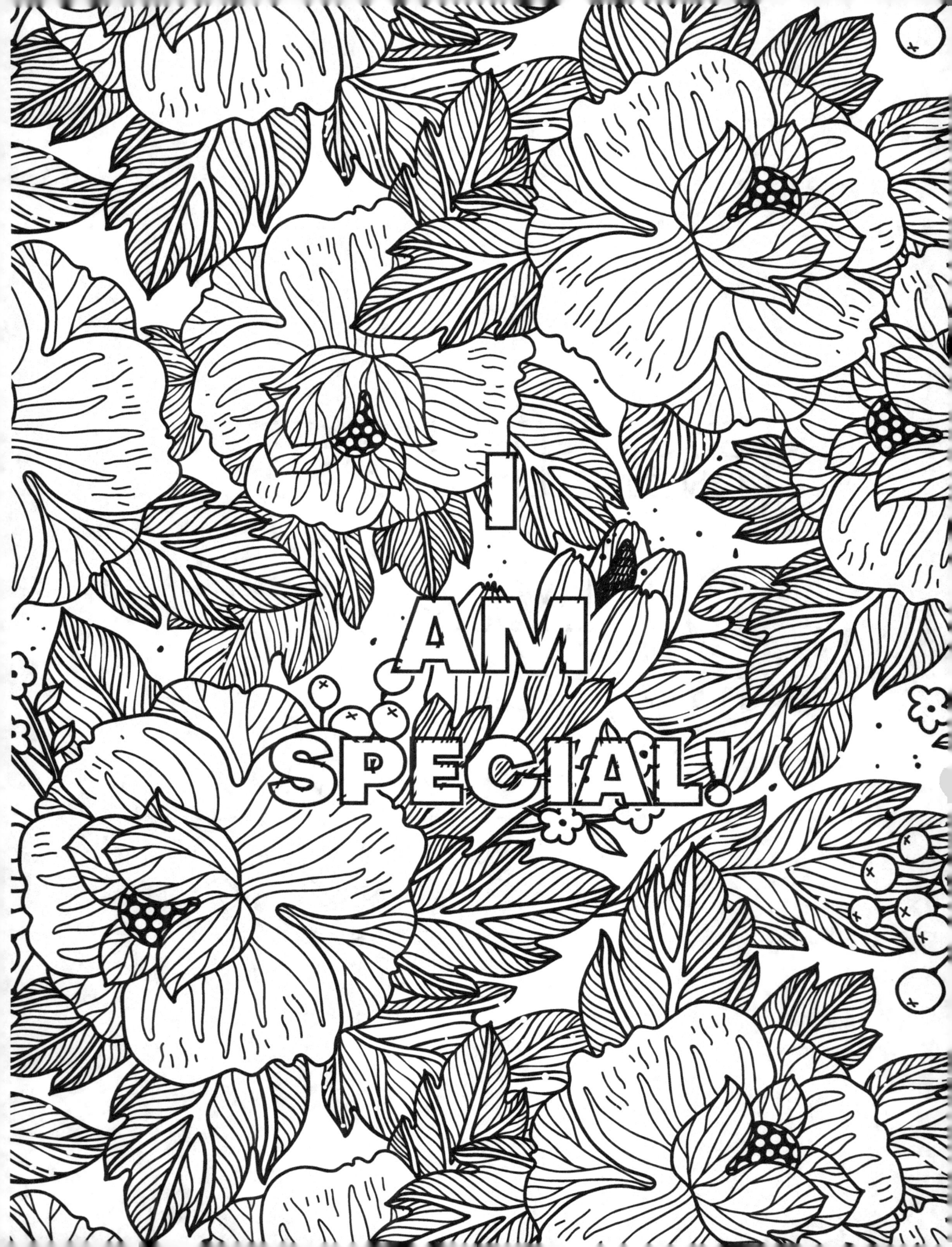

I DESERVE HAPPINESS!

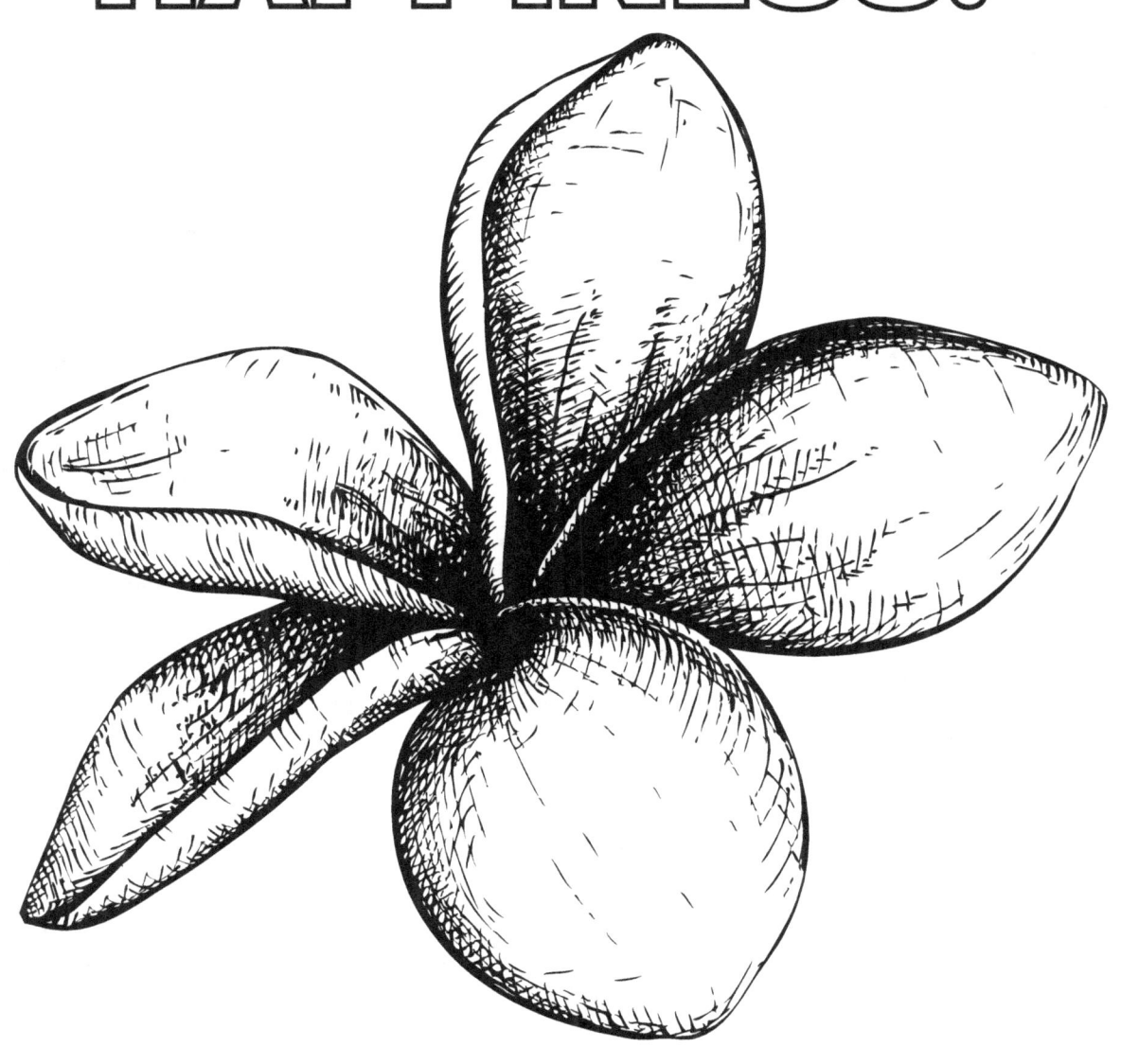

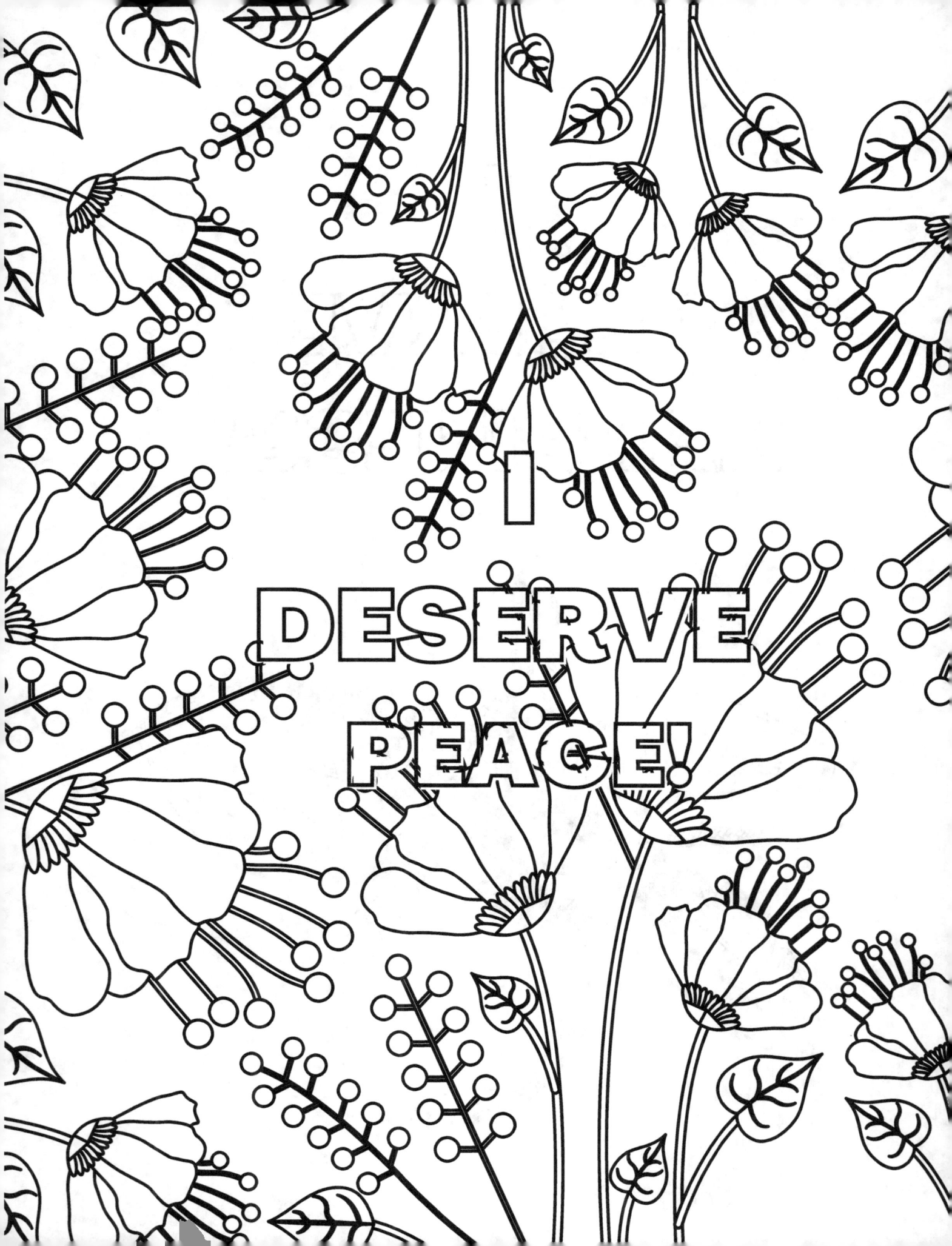

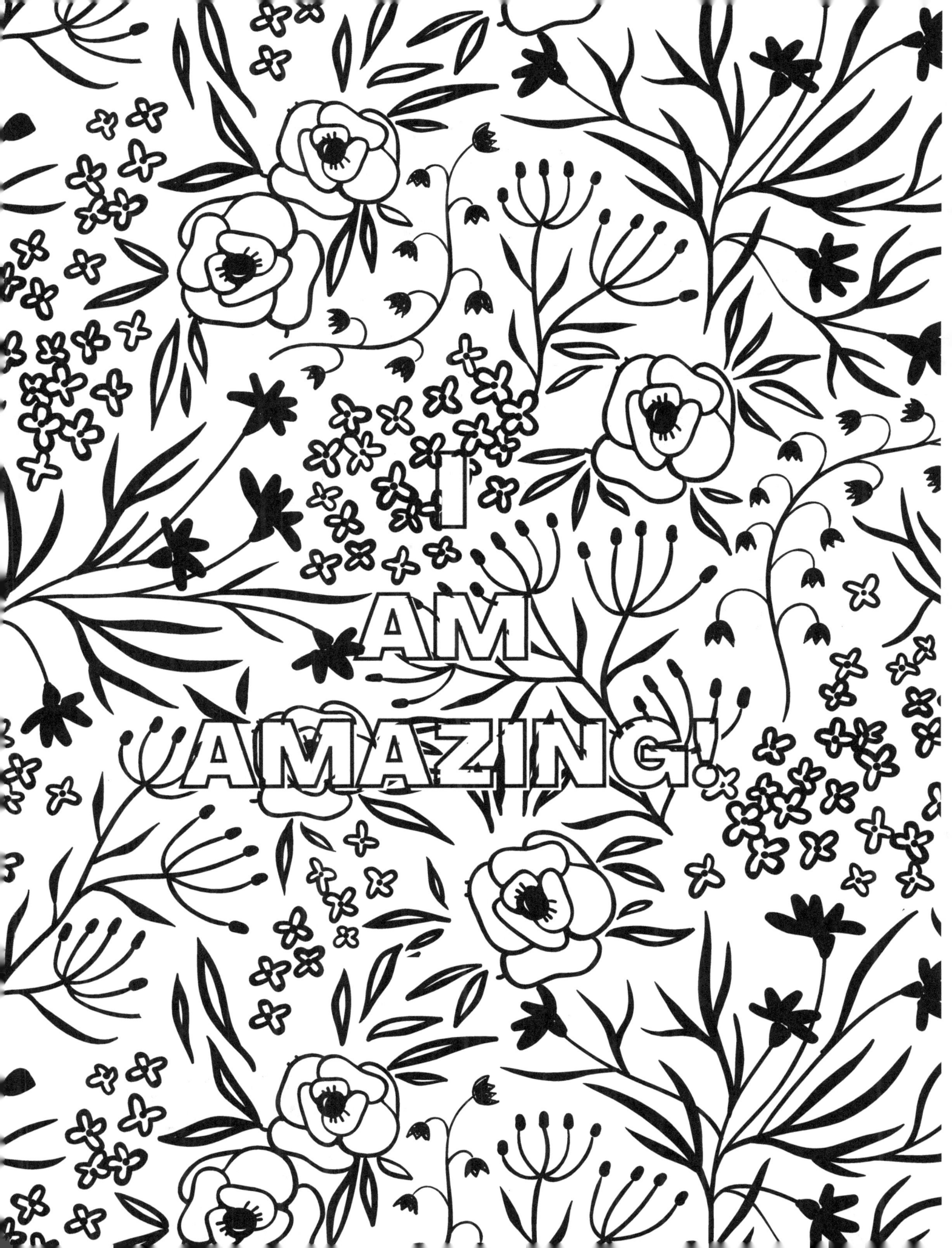

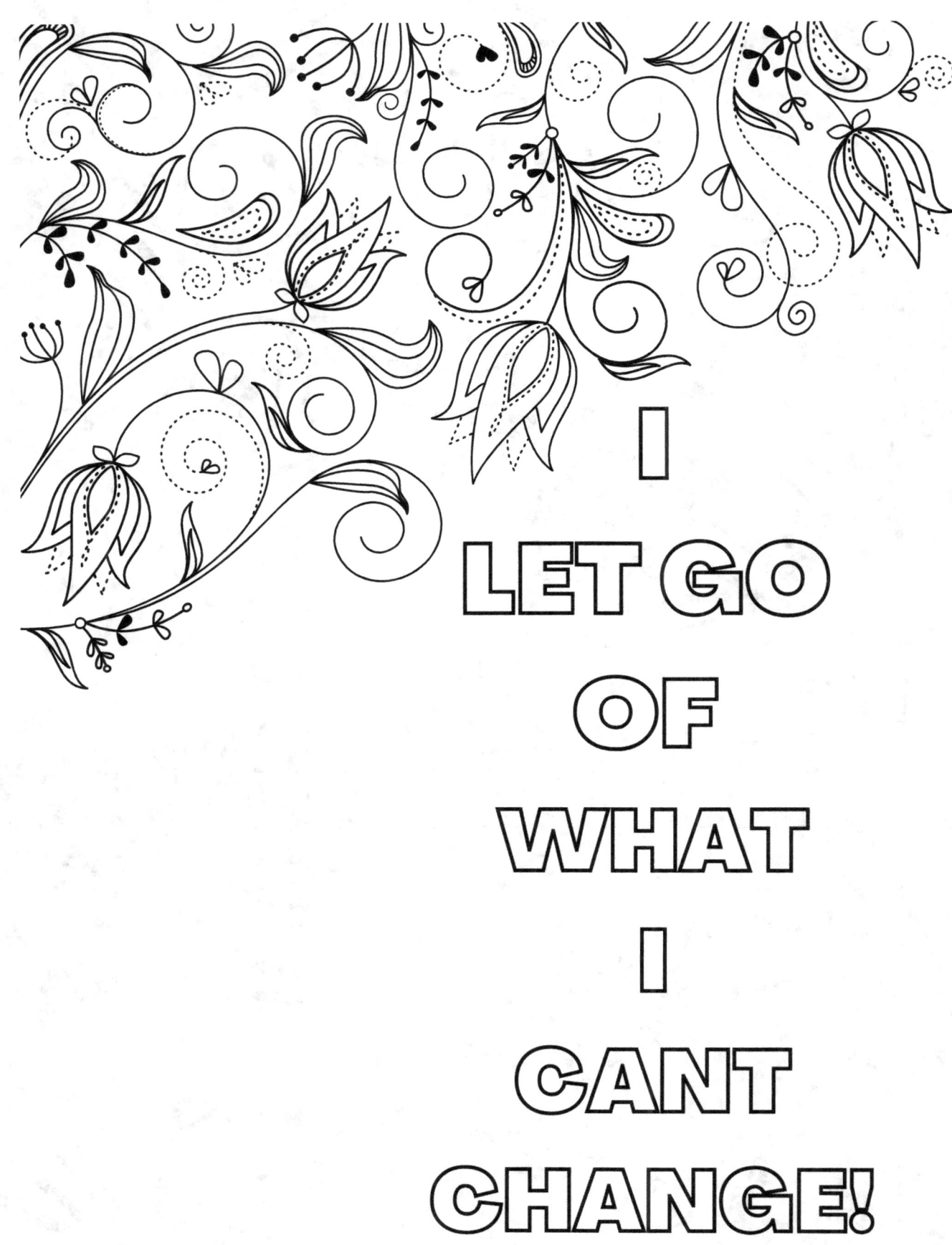

I AM AT PEACE!

I WILL KEEP TRYING!

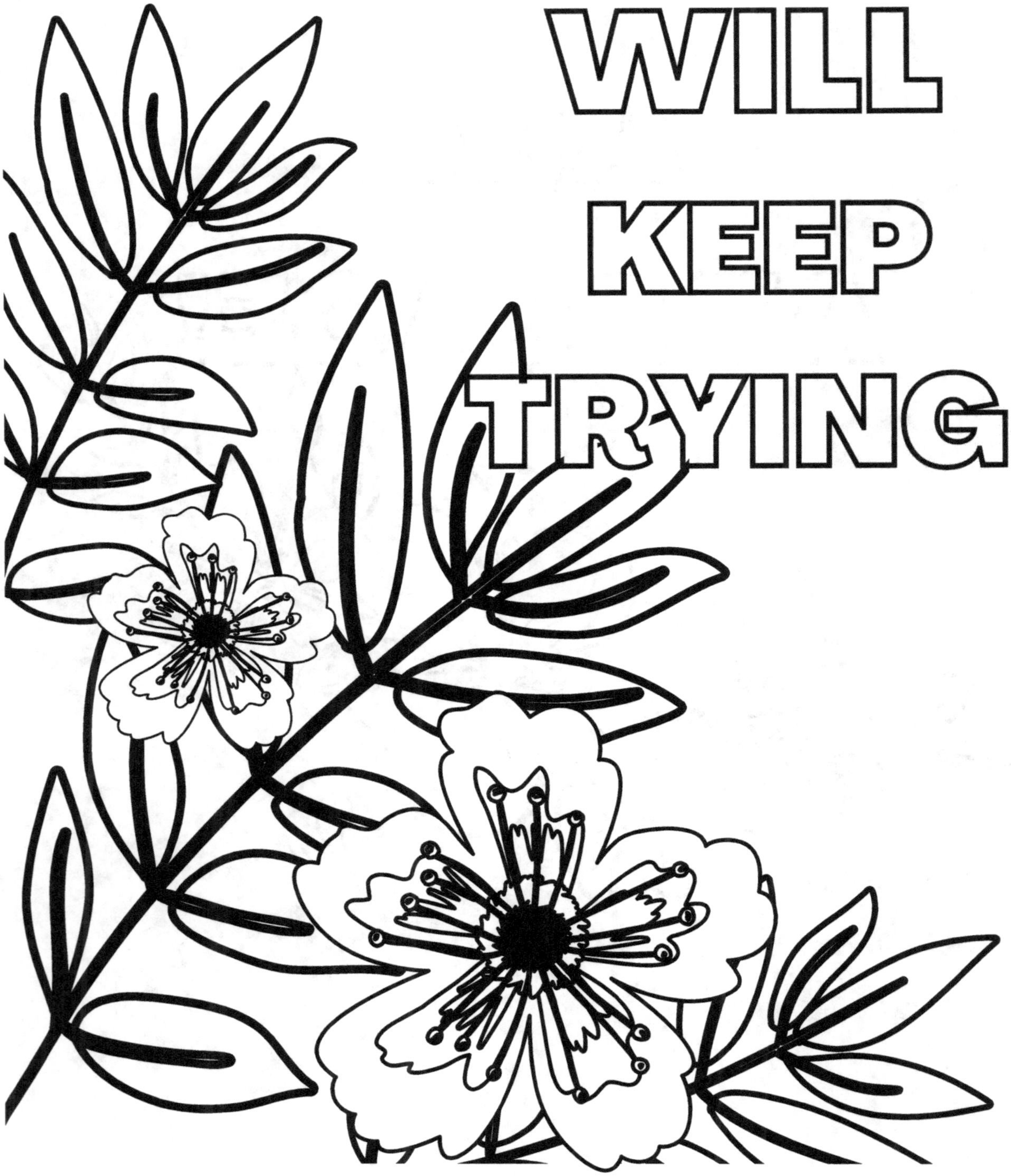

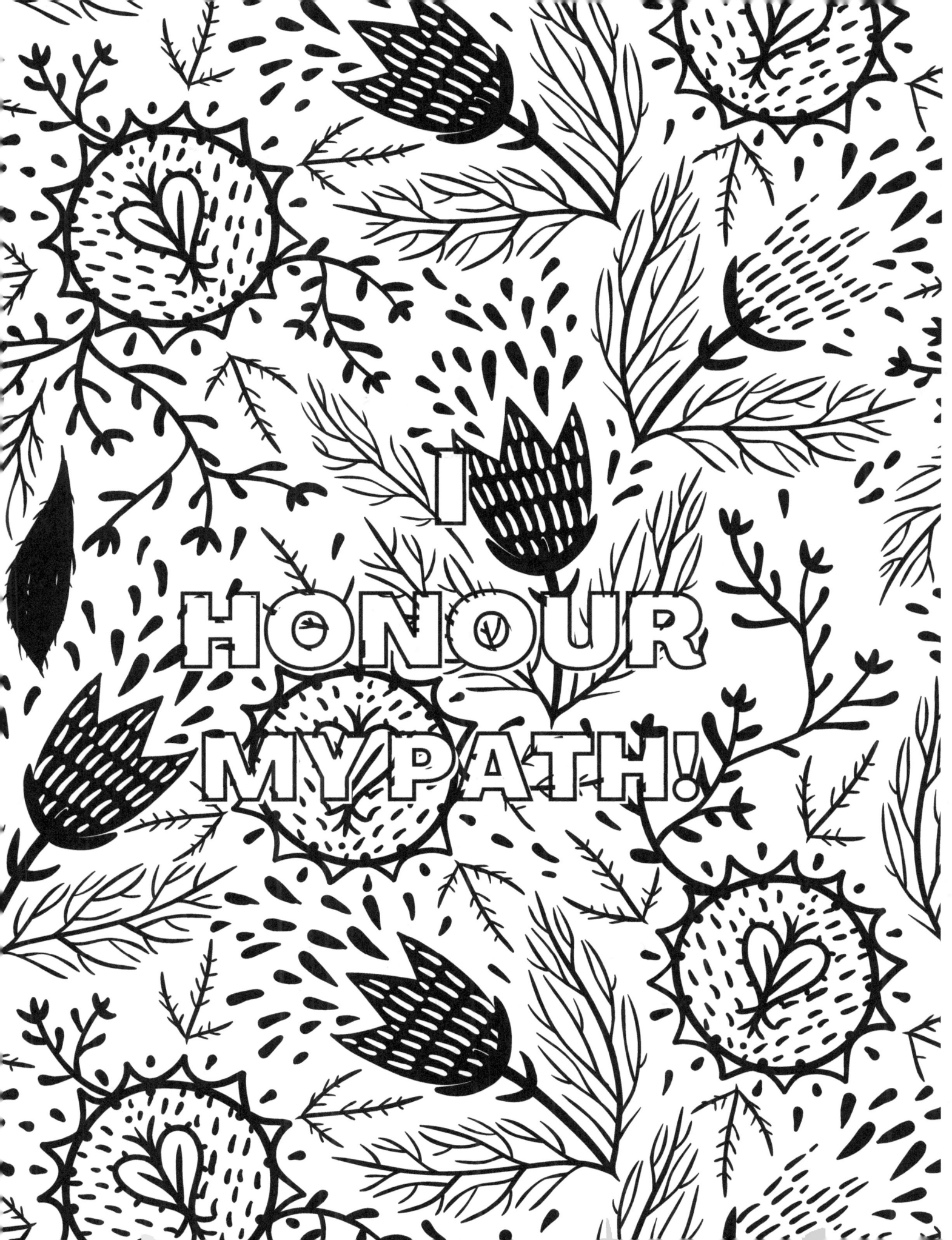

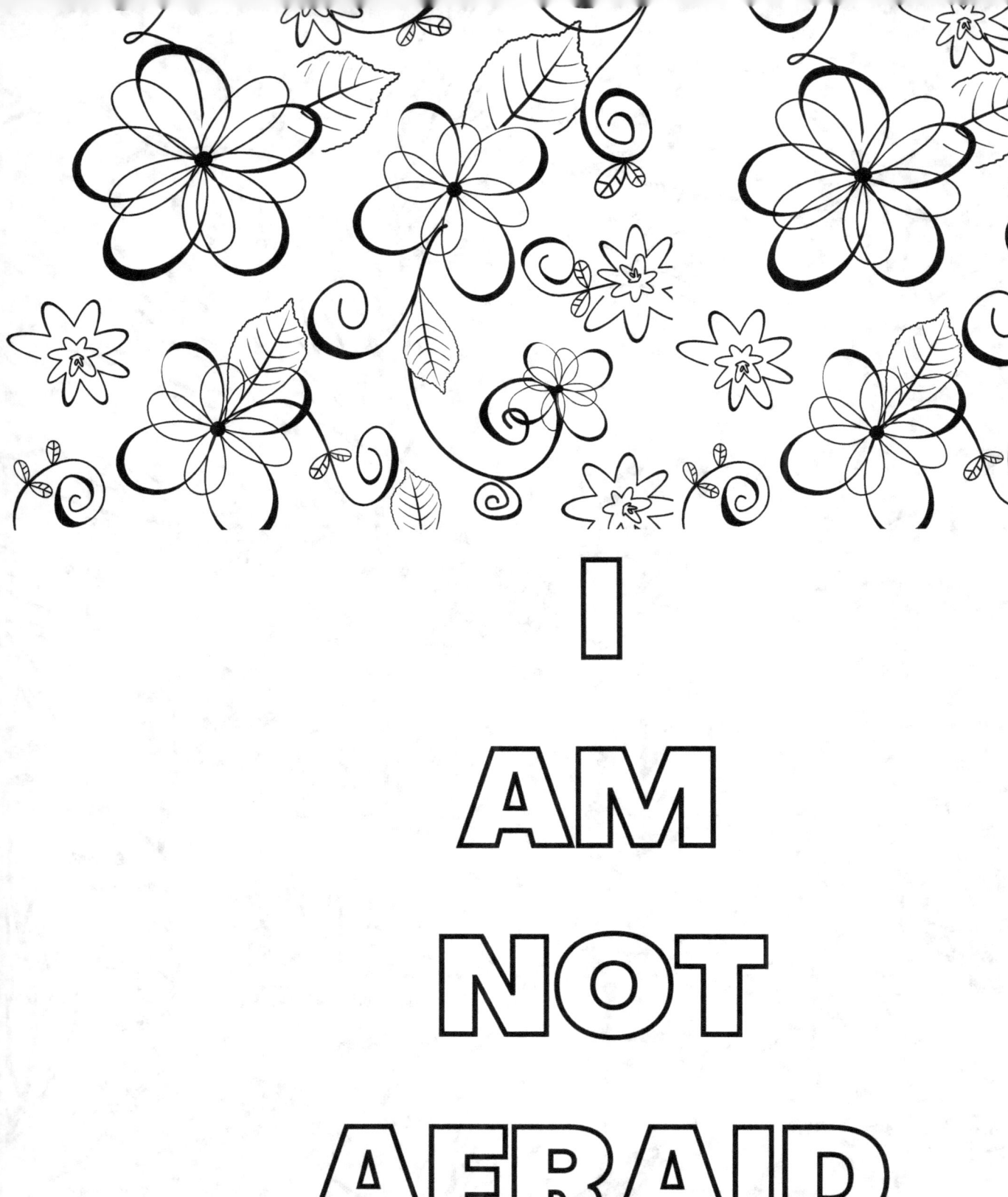

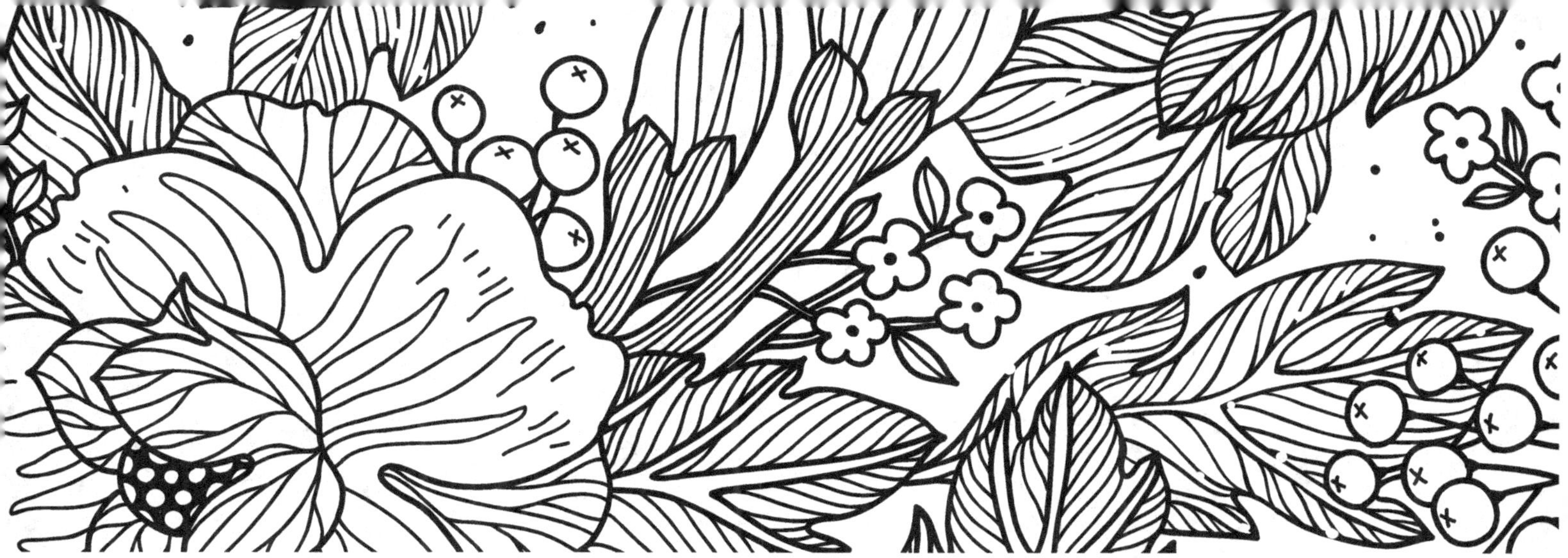

I AM GROWING WISER!

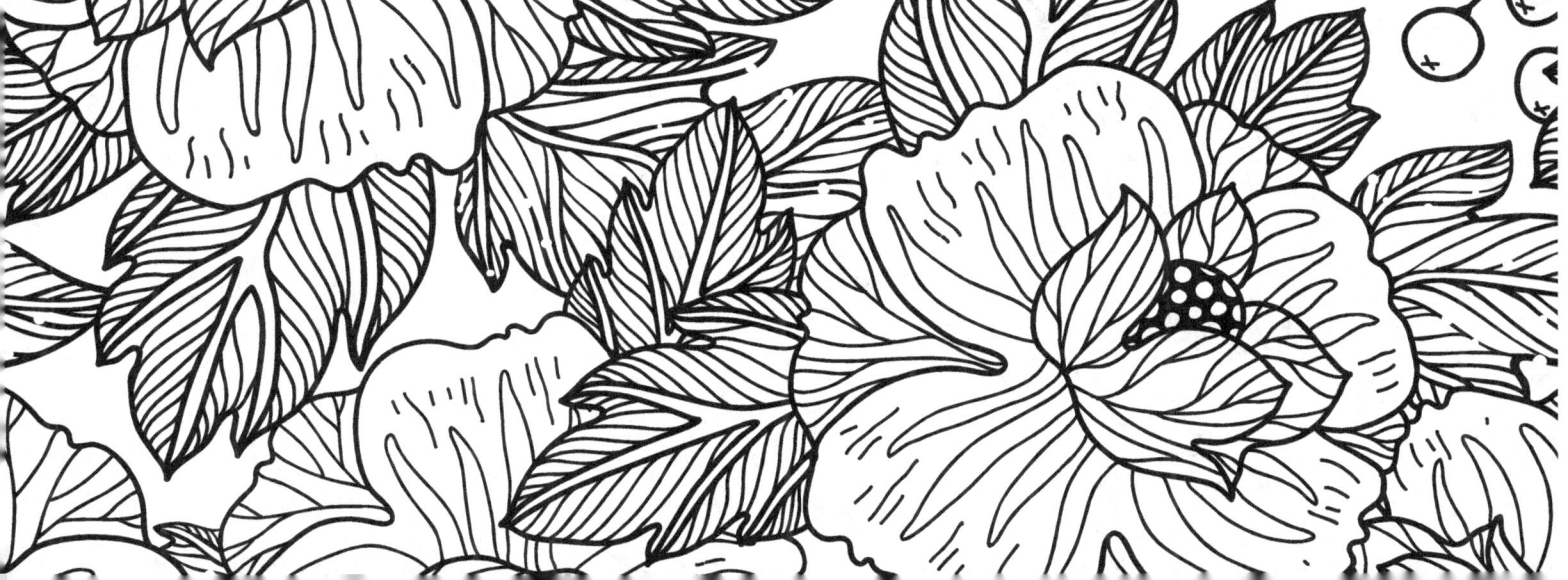

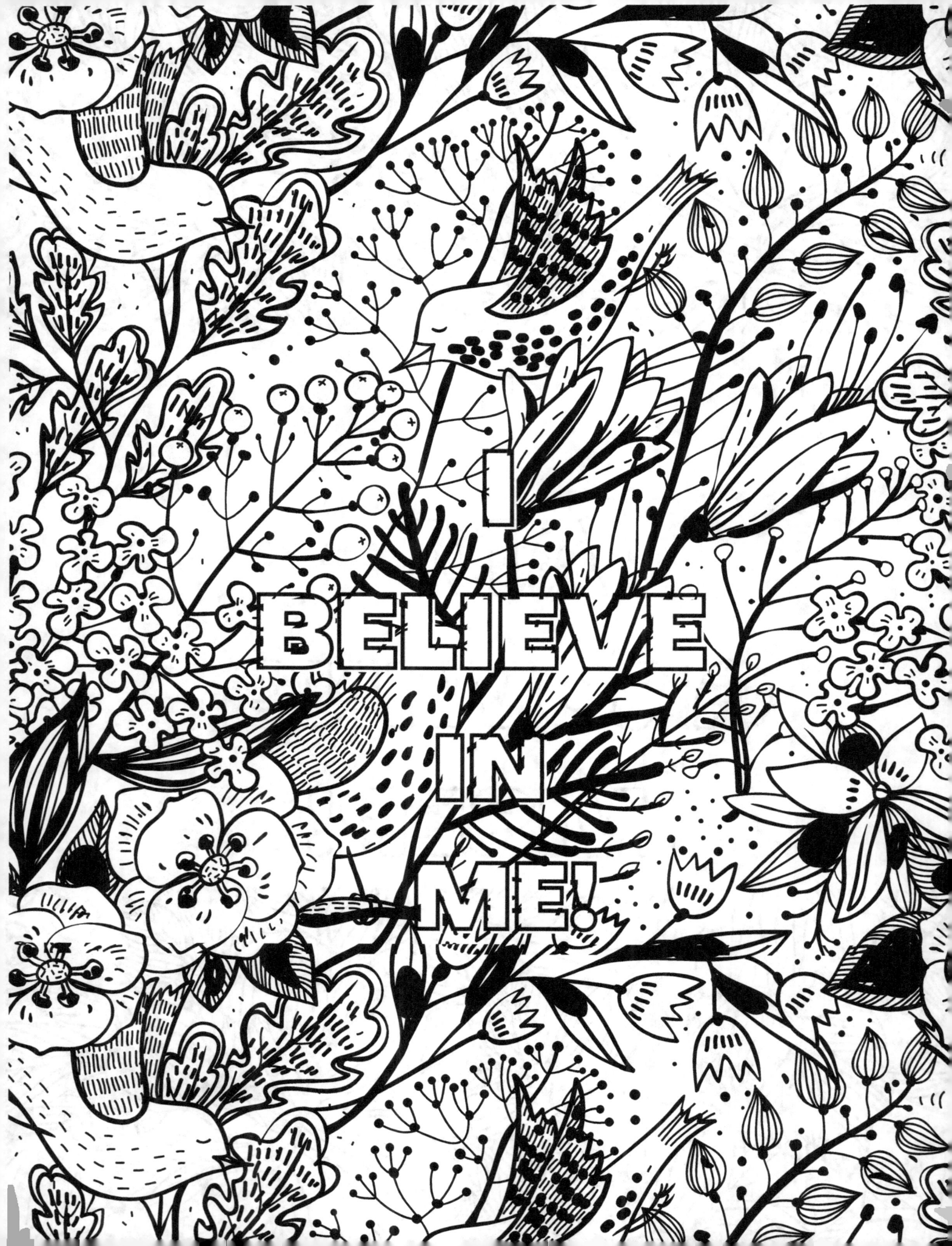

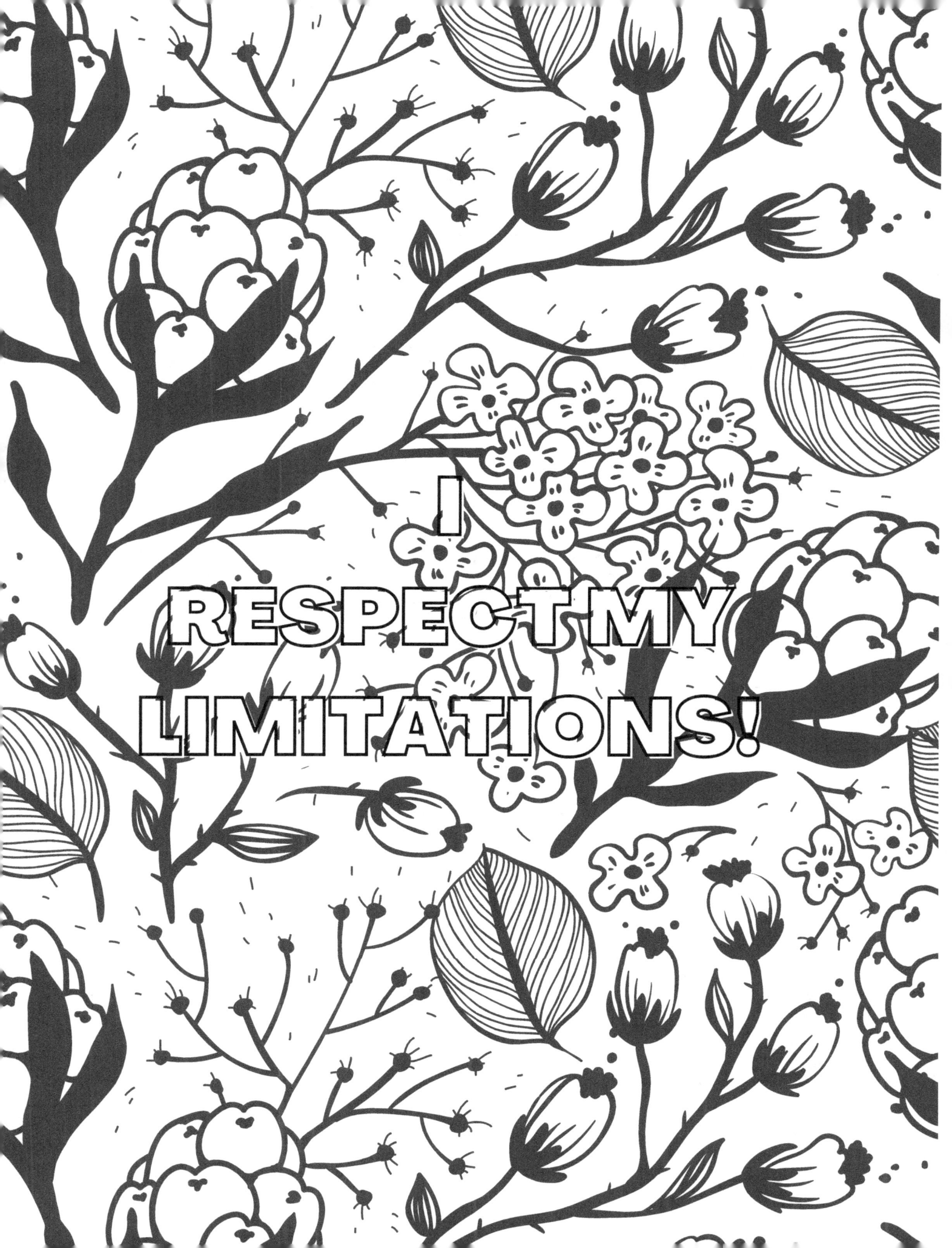

I
AM
GRATEFUL FOR
MY
CAPABILLITIES!

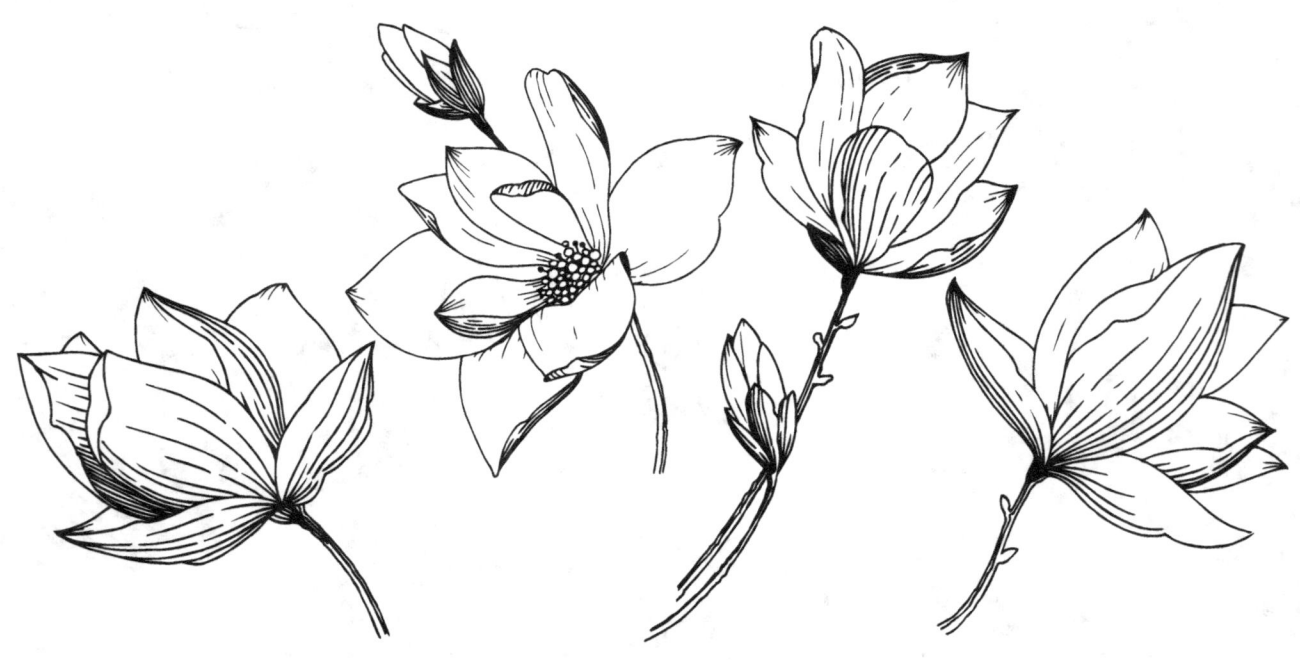

I FEEL GOOD IN MY SKIN!

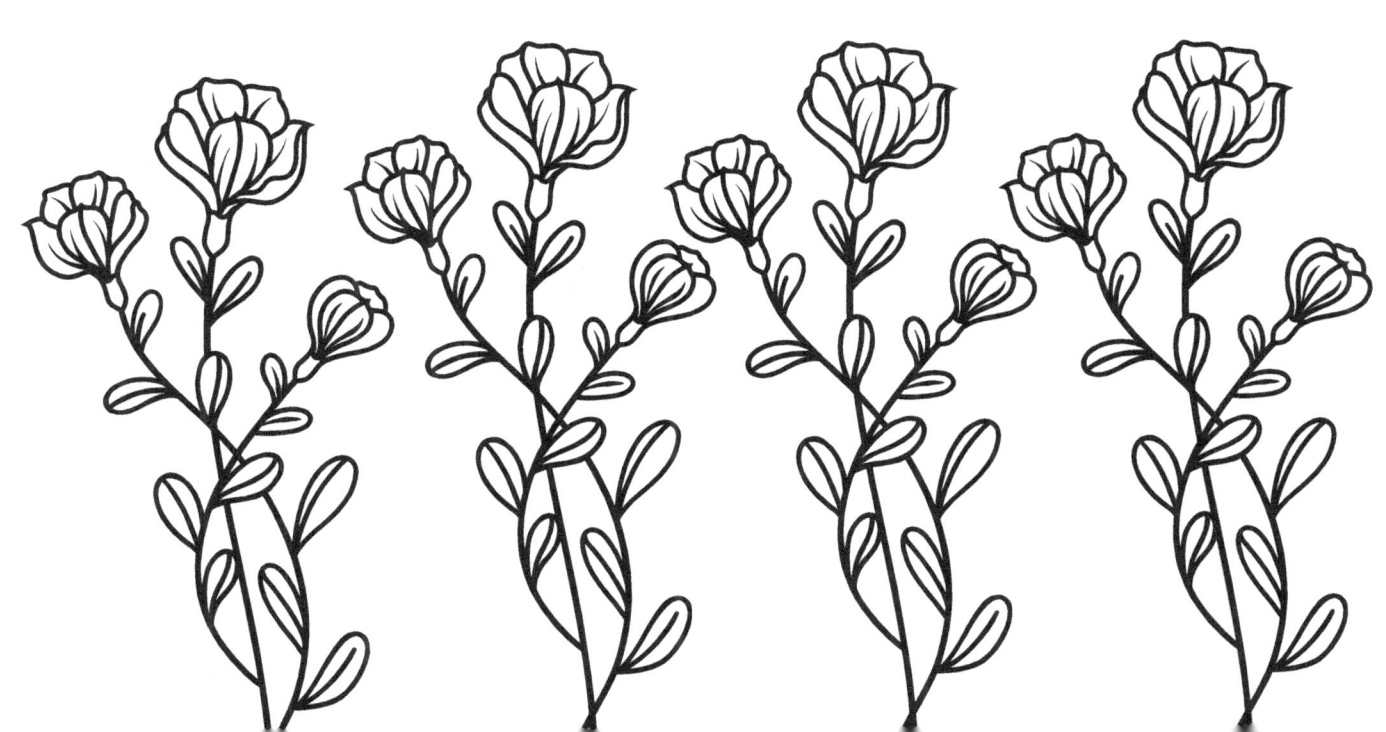

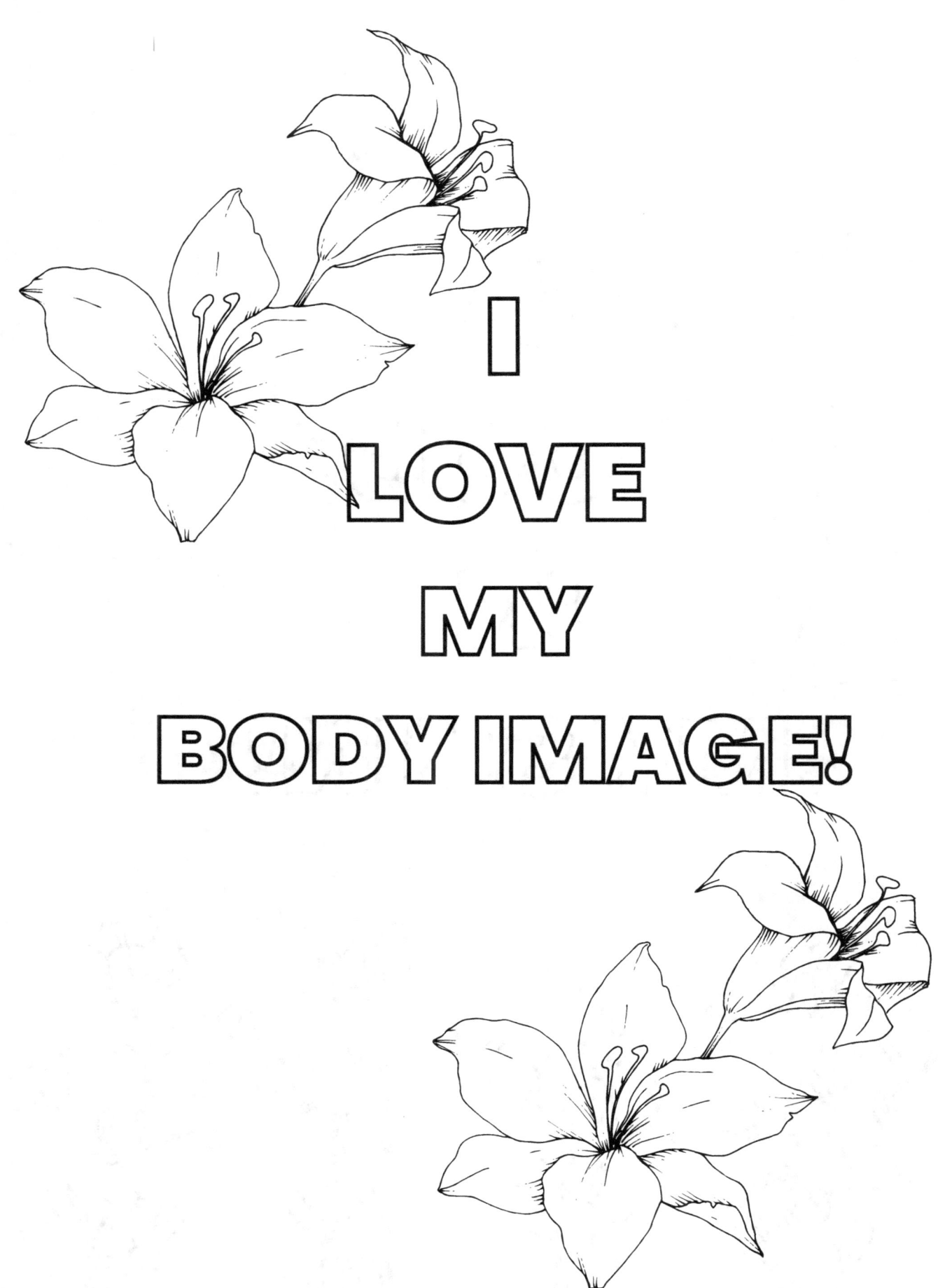

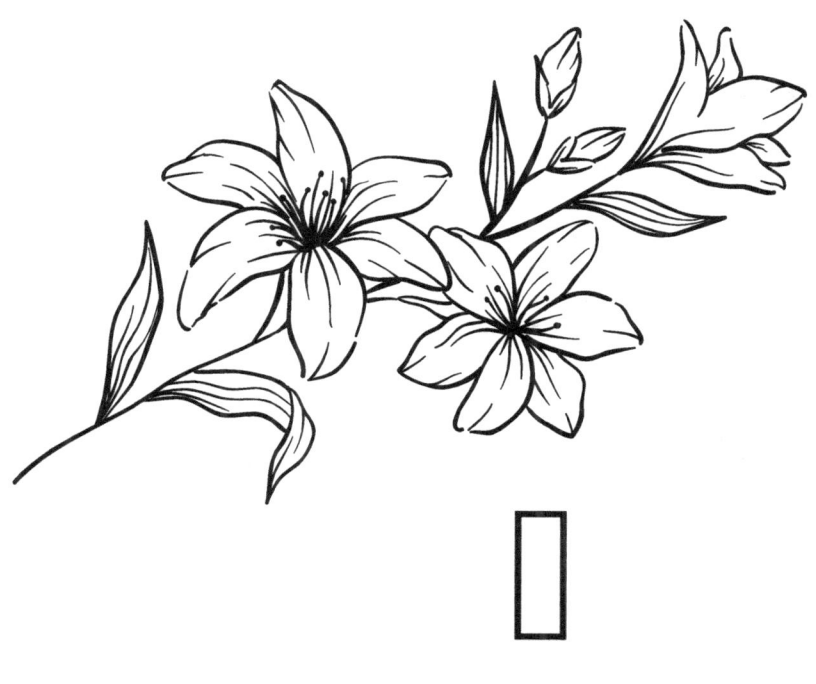

I AM WHOLE!

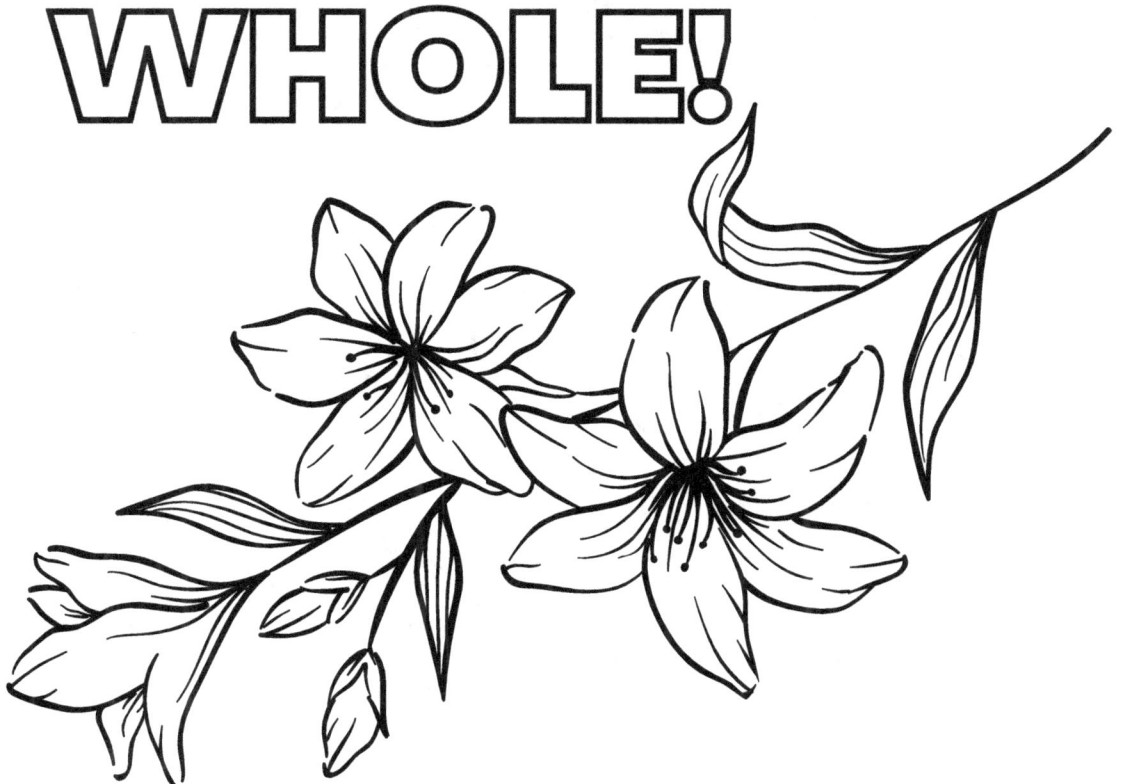

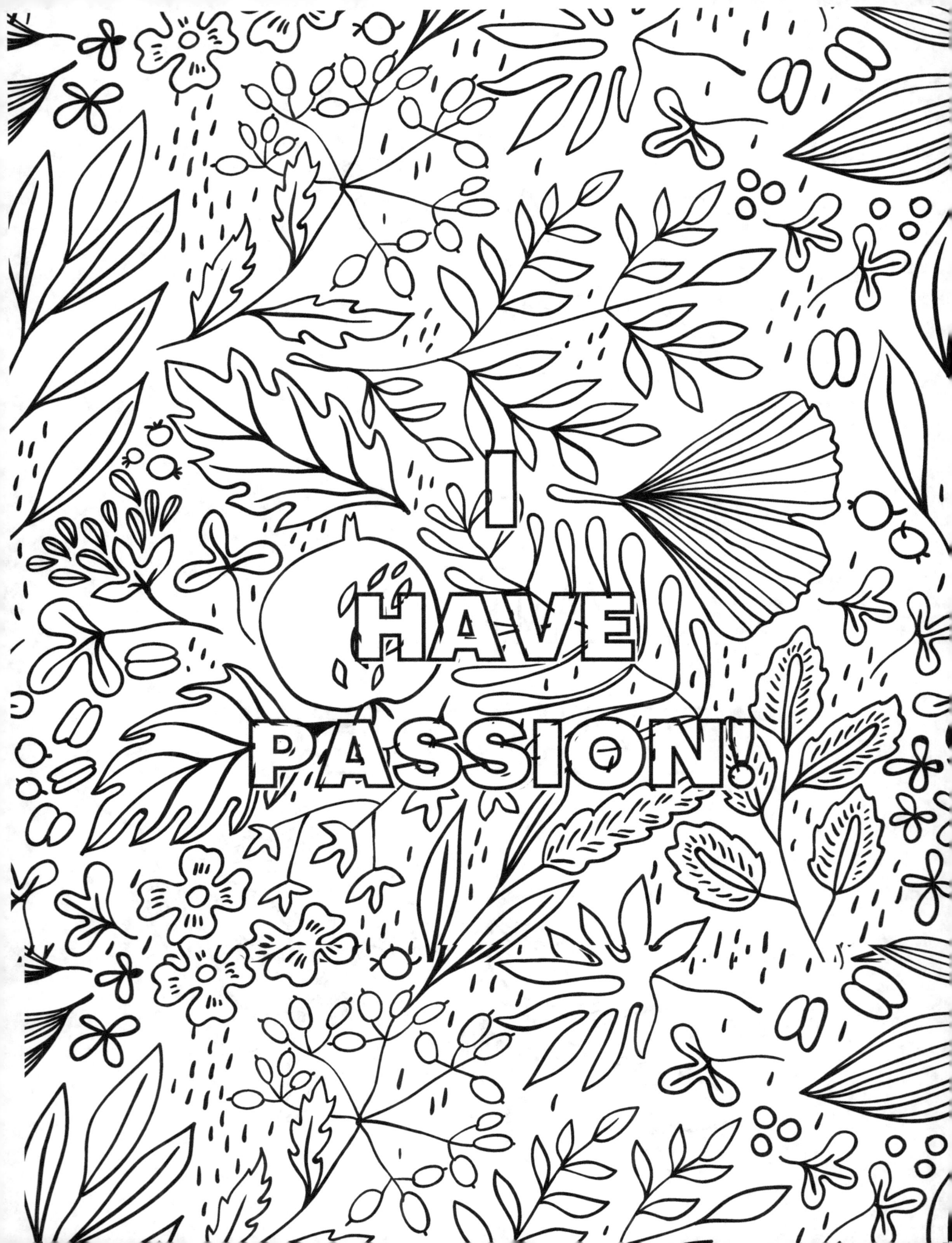

I OVERCOME

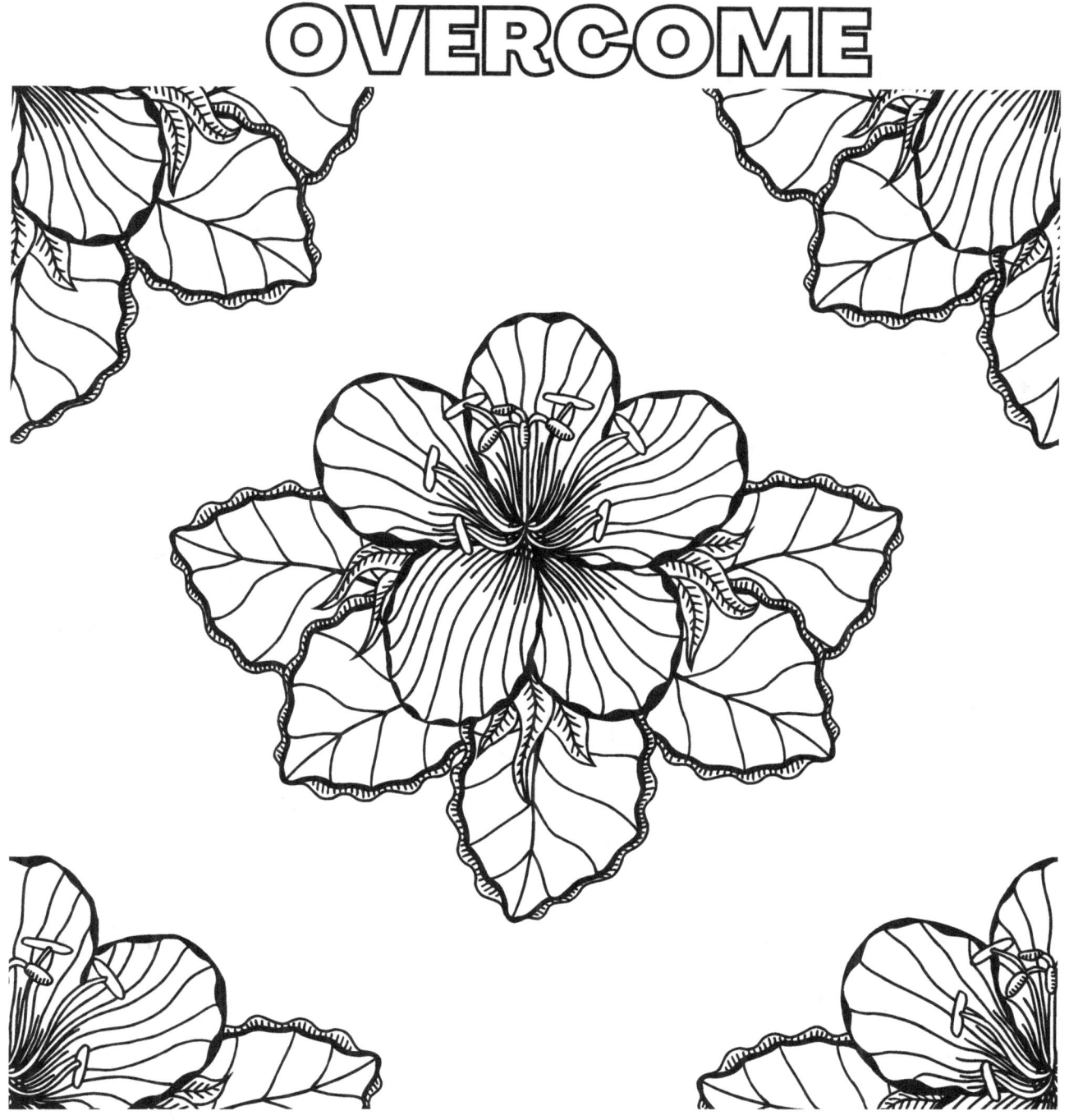

CHALLENGES!

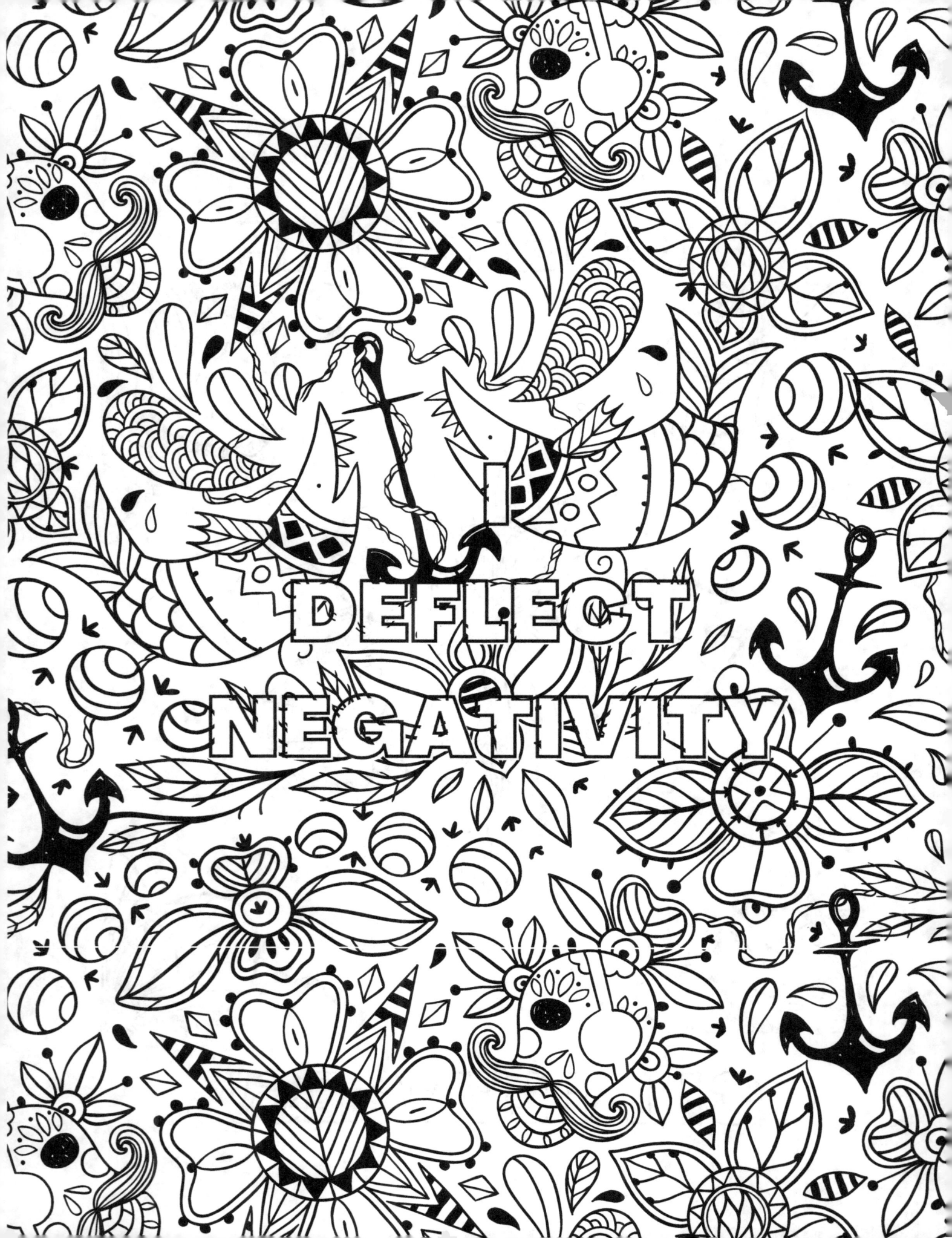

I CHOOSE TO STOP APOLOGIZING FOR BEING ME!

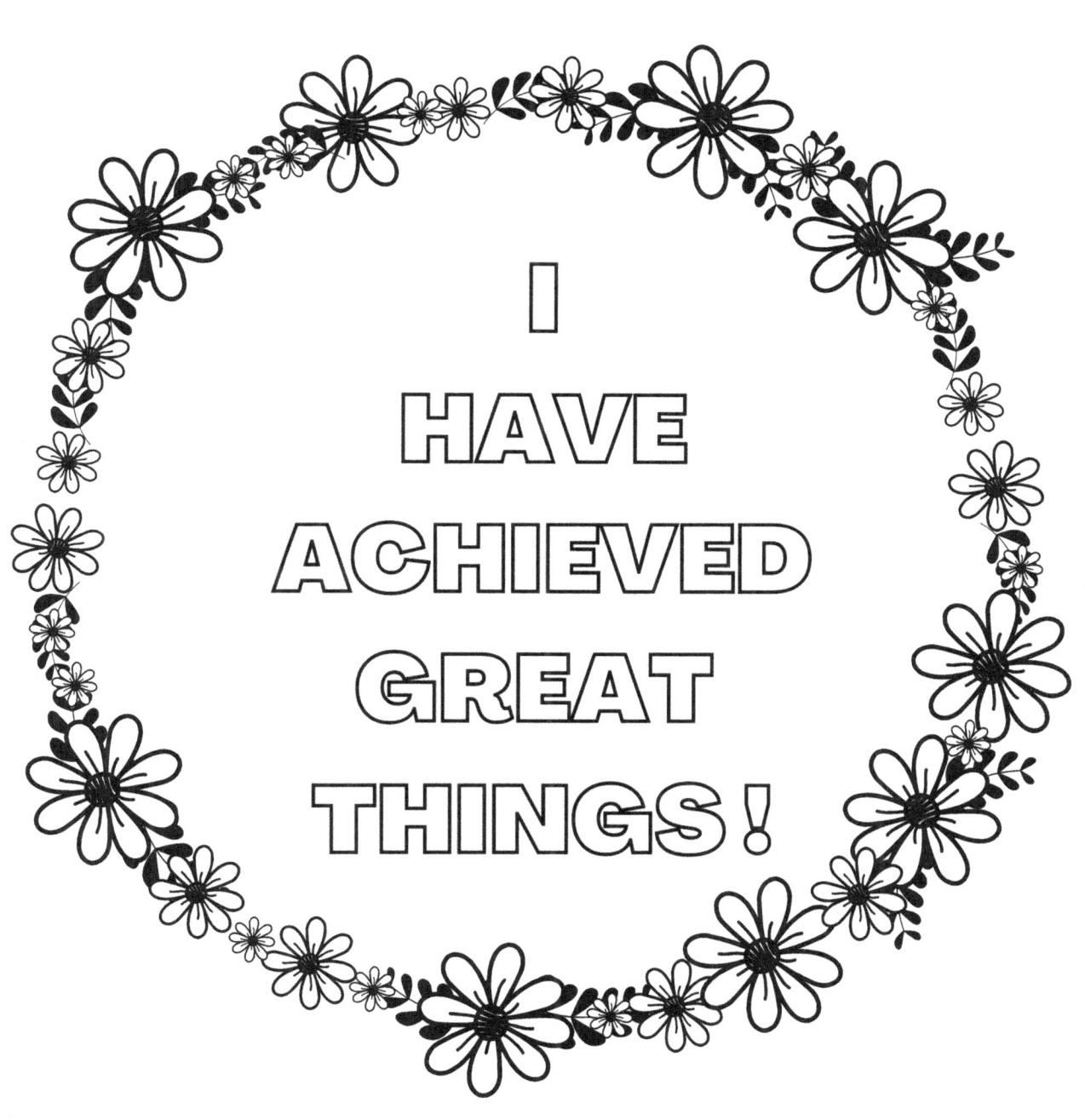

I LET LOVE IN!

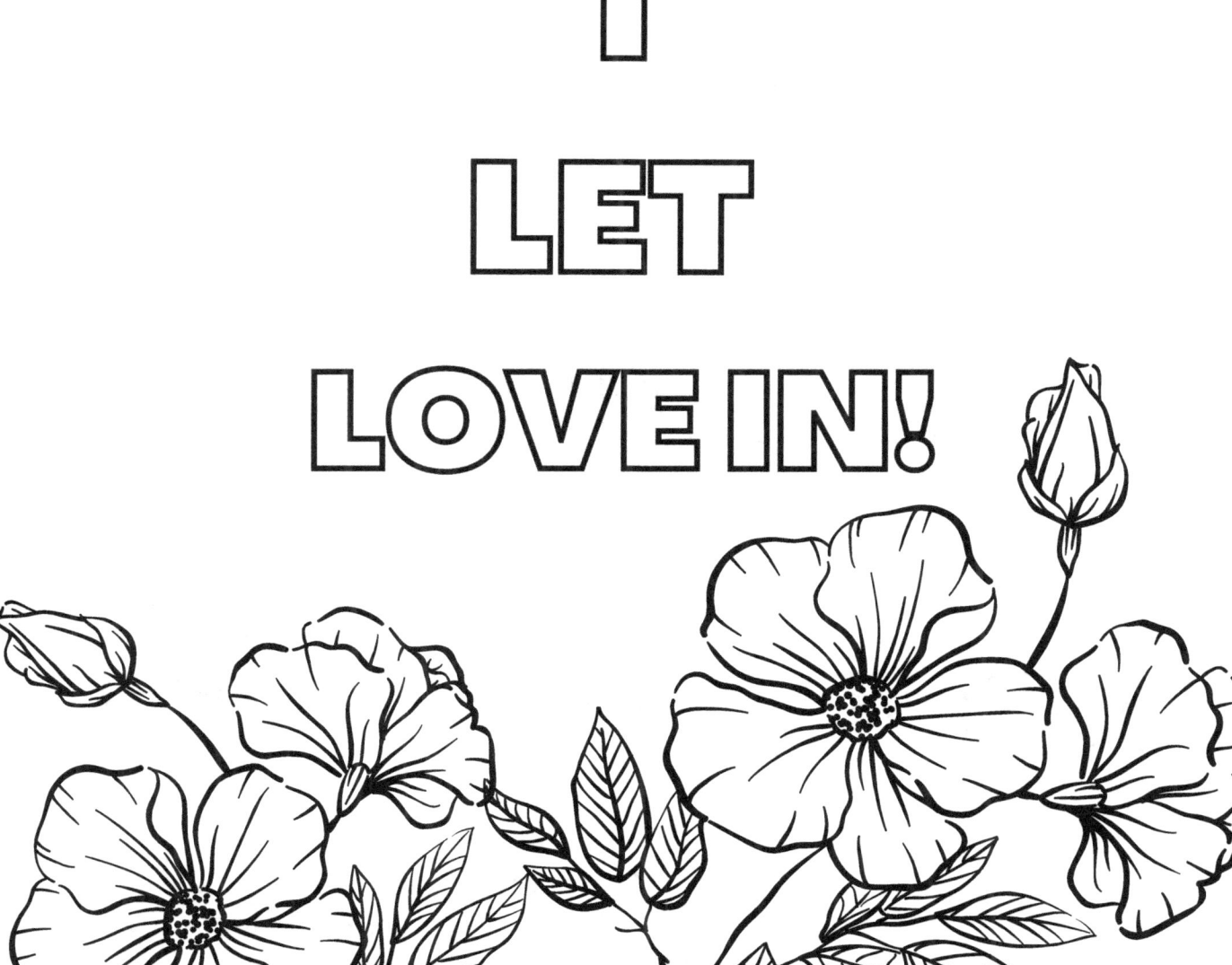

I AM CAPABLE OF GREATNESS!

I WAS
I AM
I WILL
BE GREAT!

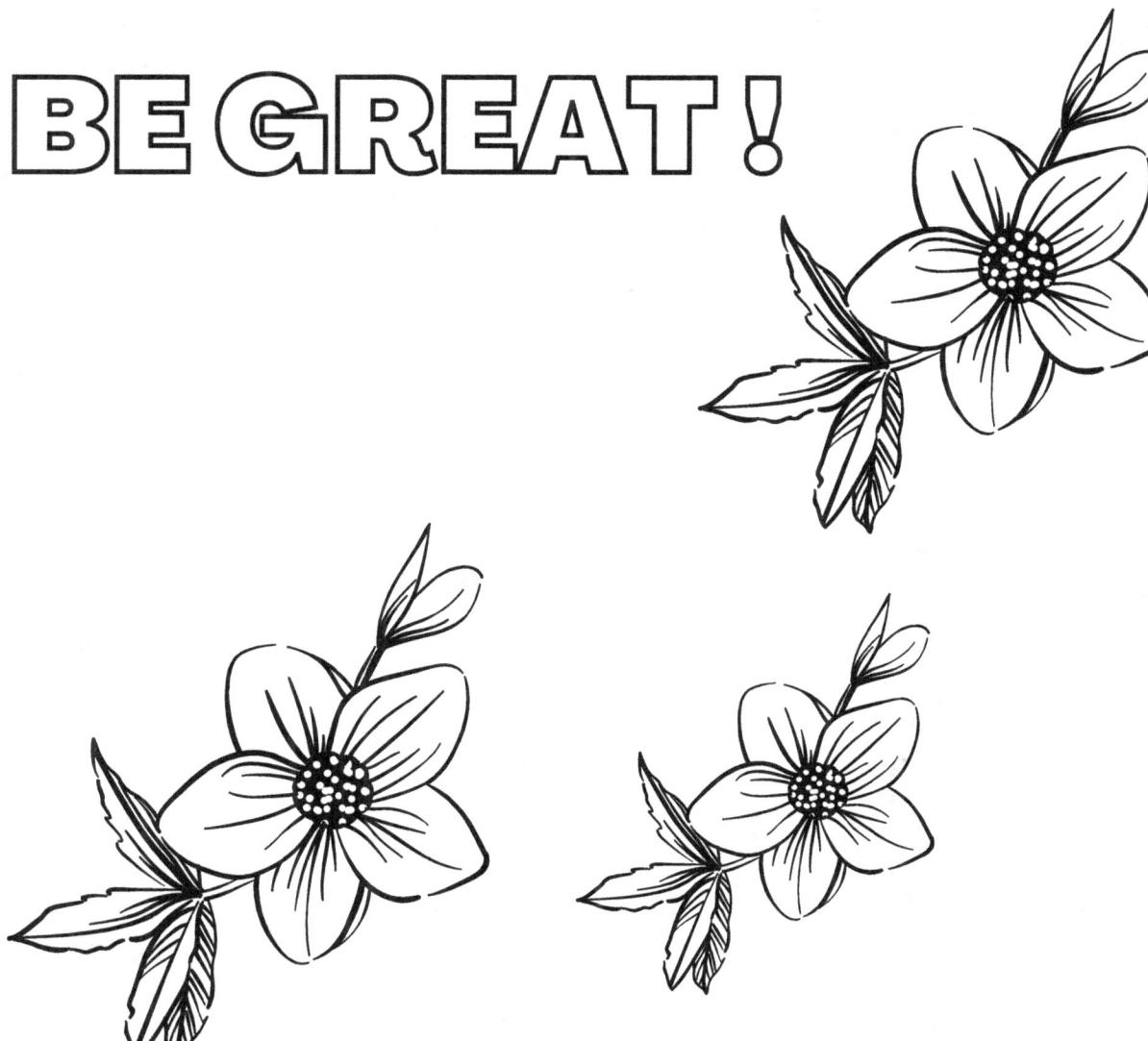

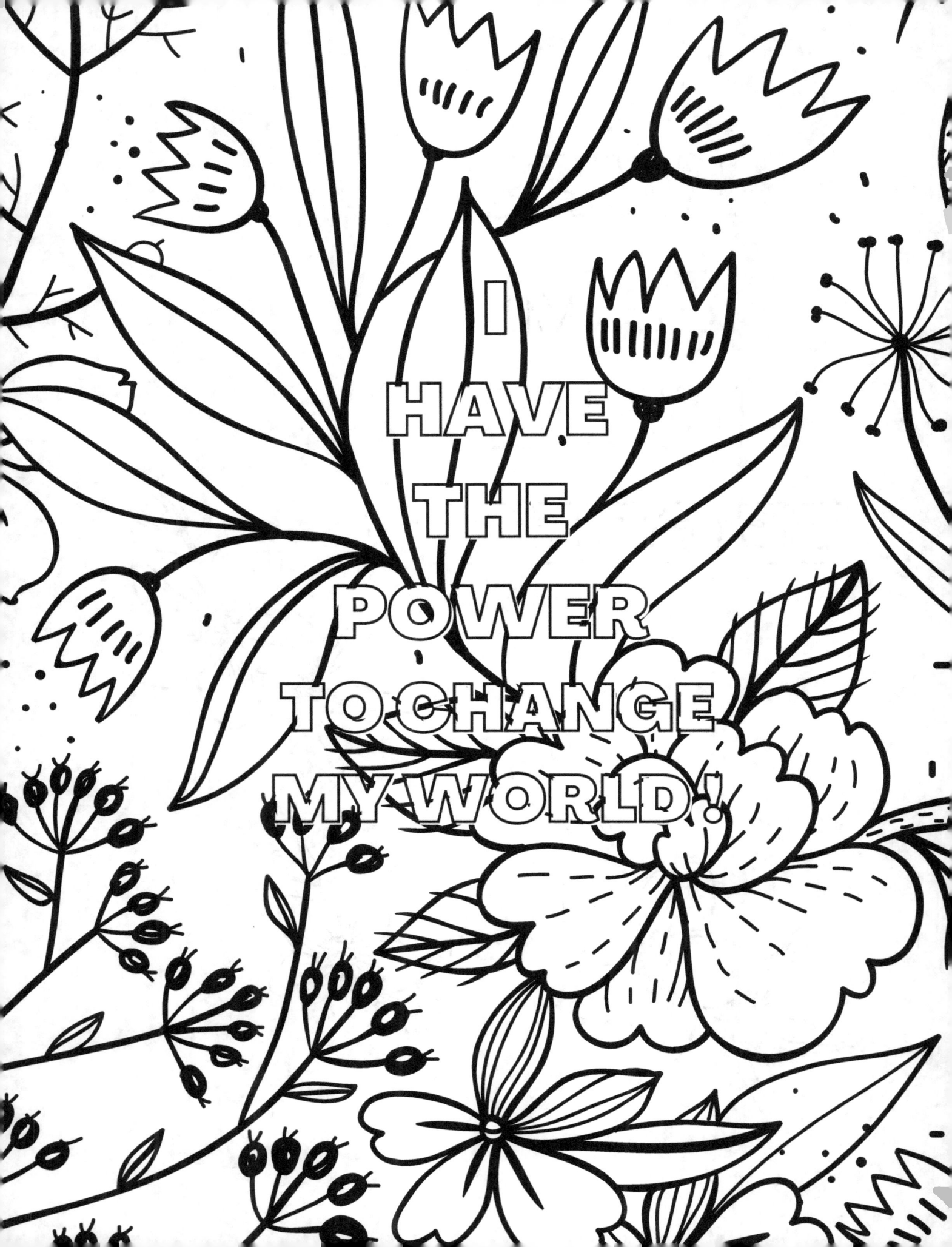

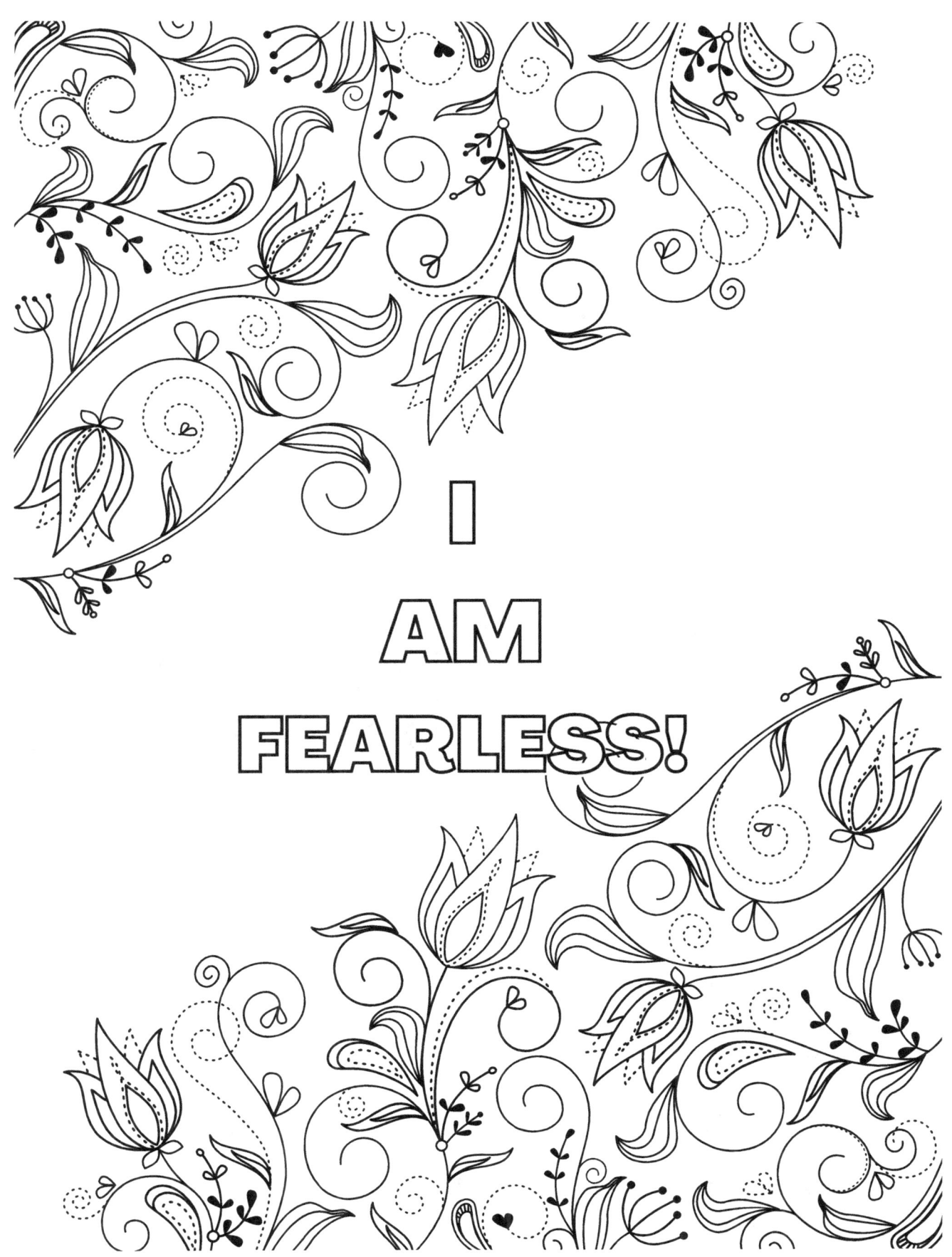

I AM CAPABLE!

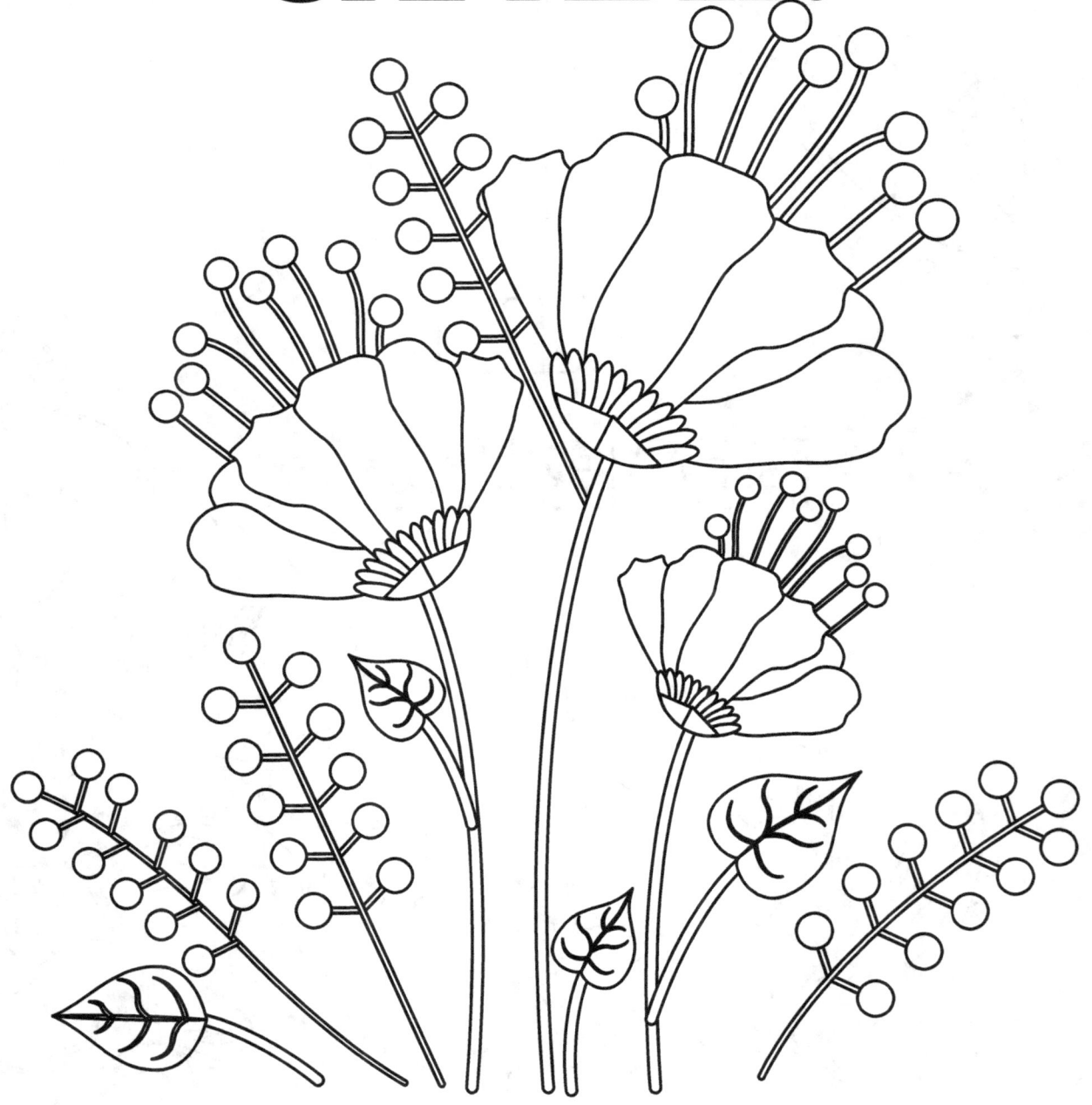

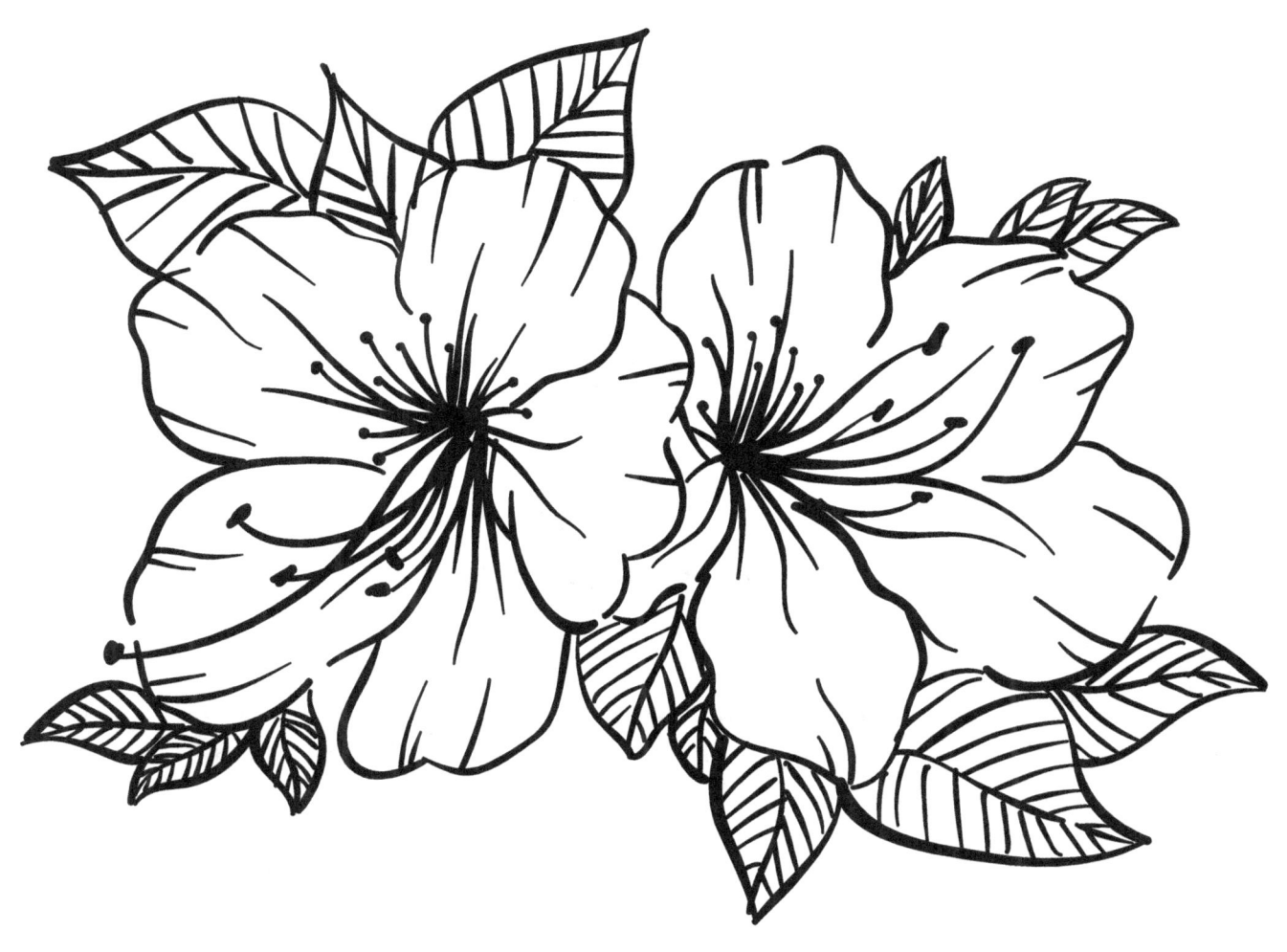

I AM COURAGEOUS!

I AM USEFUL!

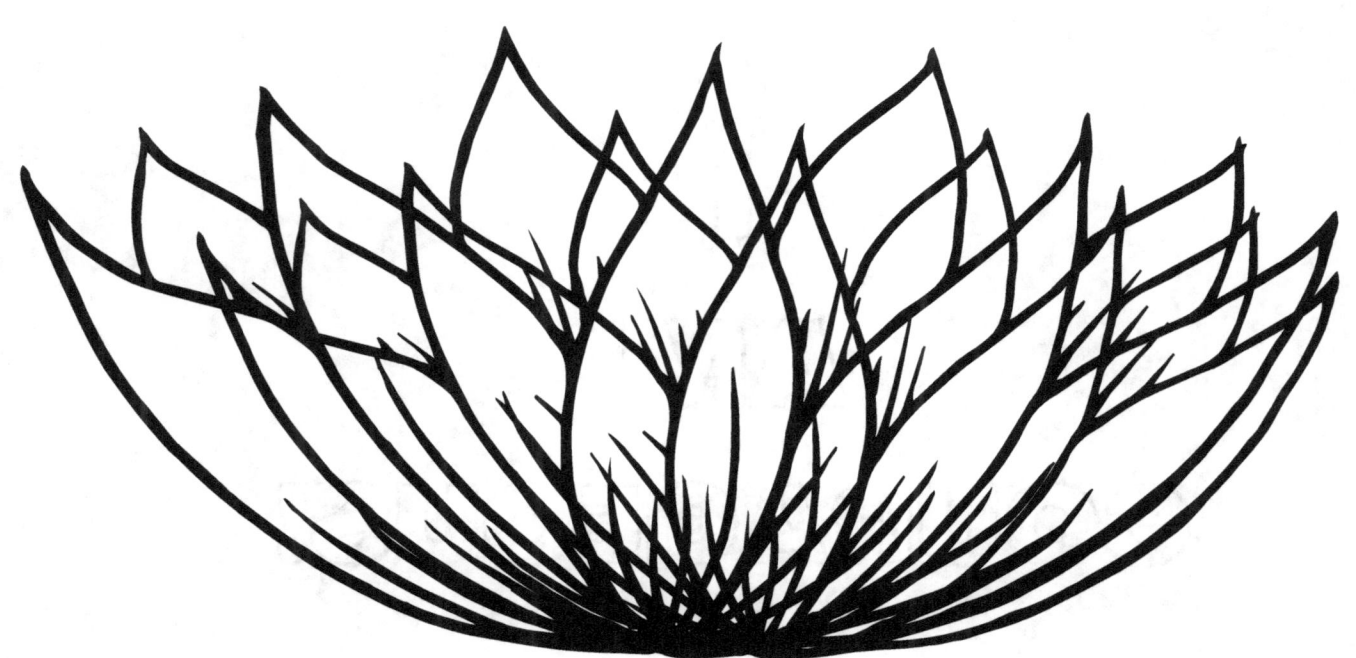

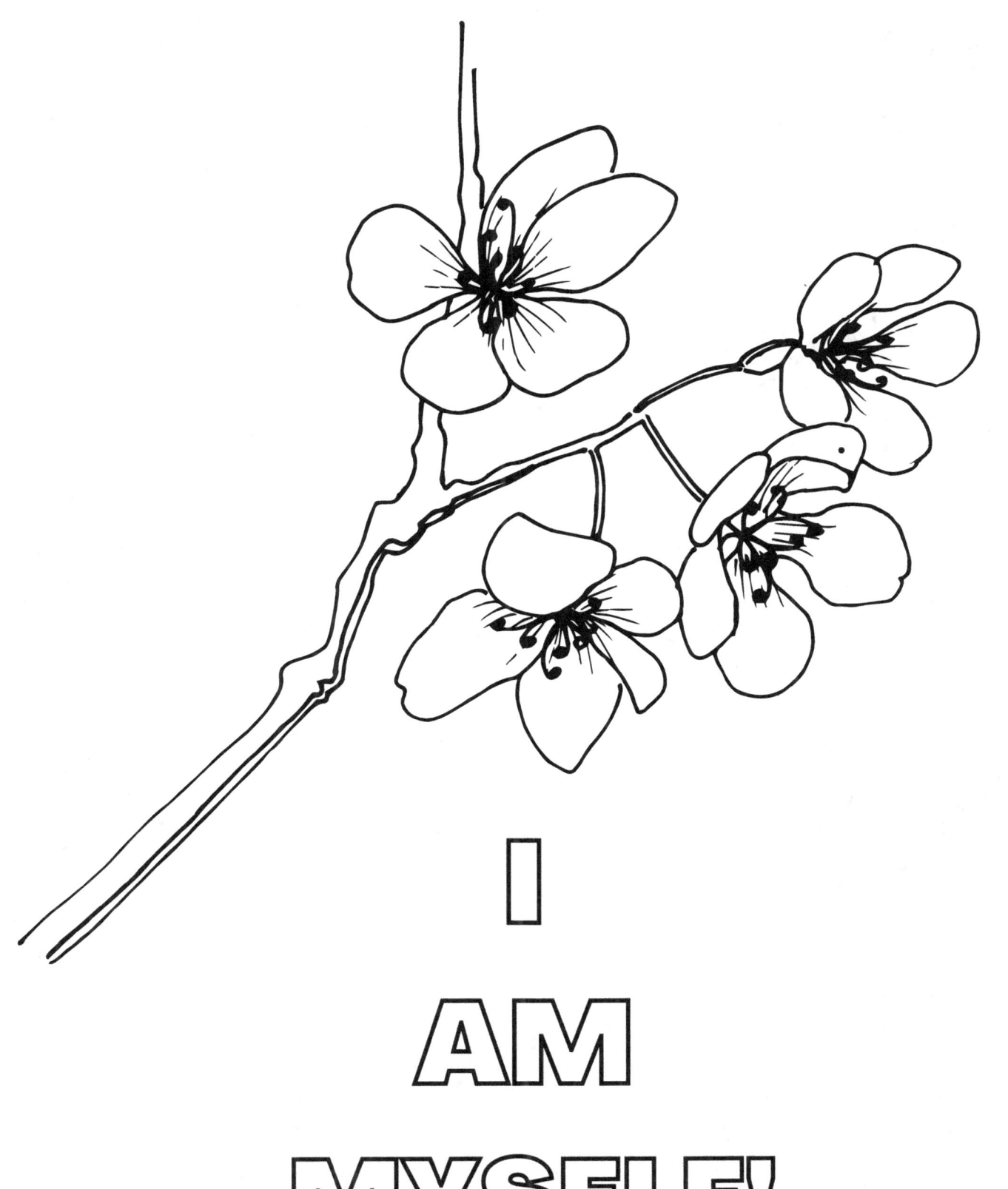

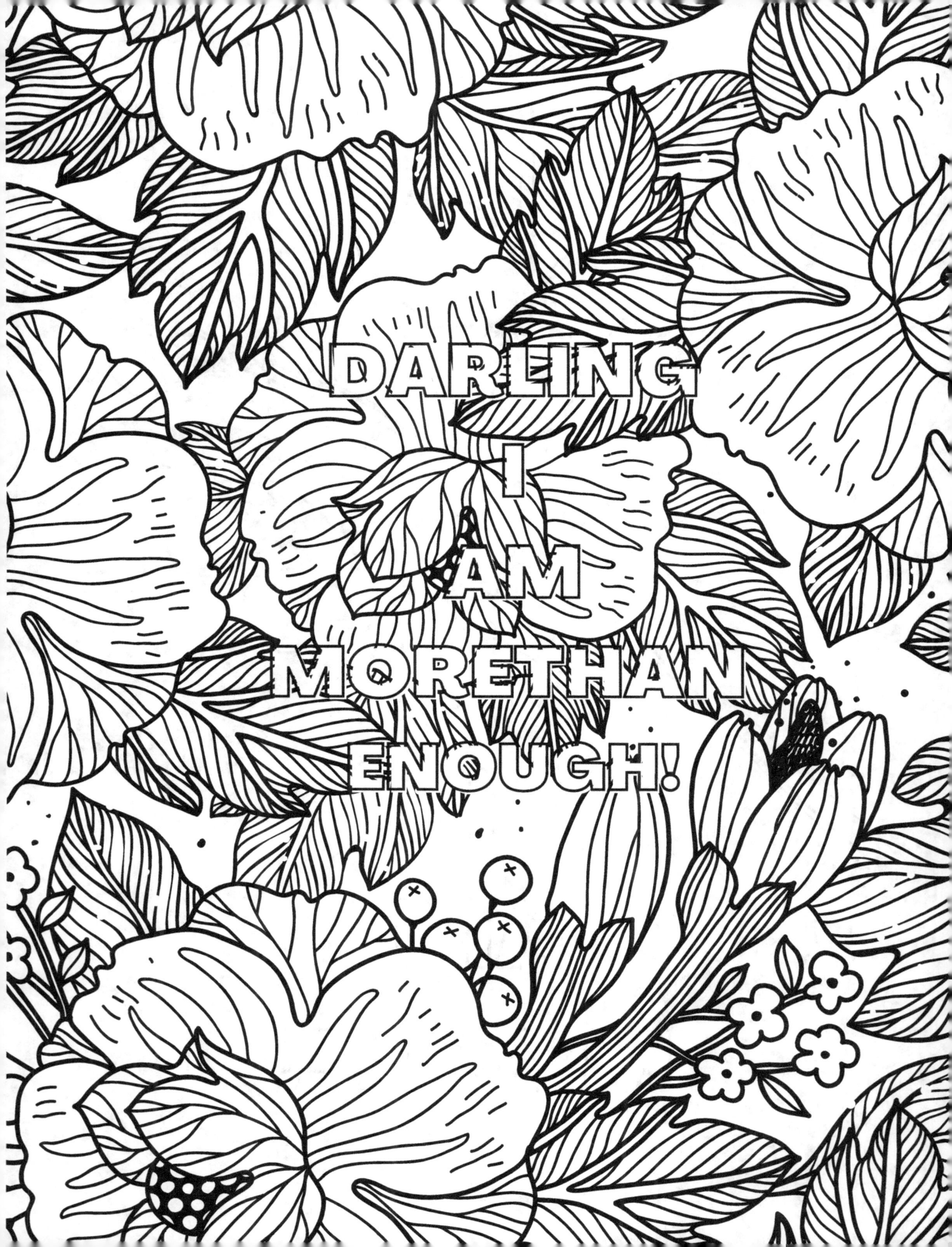

www.ingramcontent.com/pod-product-compliance
Lightning Source LLC
Chambersburg PA
CBHW080909220526
45466CB00011BA/3517